Tales of the Siren

A STARBUCKSMELODY

Melody Overton

For information contact:

Melody Overton

www.starbucksmelody.com

Cover design by Sandy Nelson, http://www.sandynelsondesign.com

Editing and book layout by Patricia D. Eddy, http://www.pdeddy.com

First Edition: May 2014

10 9 8 7 6 5 4 3 2 1

Dedication

For Jim Wood

Table of Contents

THE END

Author's Note

This book represents my own recollection of events. Most of the events described happened as related; though some were expanded and changed. Some of the individuals portrayed are composites of more than one person, and most names and identifying characteristics have been changed. Where public figures (e.g., Chef Tom Douglas, Sheryl Crow, and a few others) and Starbucks senior leadership (any executive whose name appears on http://news.starbucks.com/leadership) make appearances in this book, names have *not* been changed.

This tale begins with my first in-person encounter with Starbucks CEO Howard Schultz on April 1, 2008, and ends on January 2, 2014.

Two of the principal characters in the book are Howard Schultz, CEO of Starbucks Corporation, and Cliff Burrows, President of Starbucks Americas and Europe. They're real people. You may already have heard of them. If not, I suggest you do a quick Google search for a little background on them, though you can certainly enjoy this book without doing so.

Howard Schultz has written two books: *Pour Your Heart into It* and *Onward*. In fact, *Onward* covers much of the same era as this book. The time period from 2008 through 2011 was one of rapid and unprecedented change for Starbucks, as they tried to transform their business into something new to cope with the United States' recalcitrant downturn in the economy. I think that era of rapid change, new products, and testing of new ideas, helped fuel some good stories. In fact, I doubt that this book would have many of its stories were it not for this rapid evolution of the Starbucks business happening everywhere around me. I recommend that you read *Onward*.

Since this book spans about five years, it can't possibly cover all the interesting things that happened. A few times I traveled to other cities to see what Starbucks was like there, and I had interesting and fun experiences meeting other customers, store partners, district managers, regional directors, and even a regional vice president. With all of those stories, I could have made this into a very long book, but I wanted to keep it thin. Also, for legal reasons, it's much easier to write about public figures than identifiable people.

As time progressed, I realized that some of my earliest comments and assumptions about Starbucks were wrong. There were times that it felt like the more I learned about Starbucks, the less I knew.

I'd like to thank Howard Schultz and Cliff Burrows for being great people. They made for some great stories. More importantly, they're responsible (along with everyone who wears the green apron) for bringing the Starbucks experience to life, and ensuring a sustained and enduring Starbucks business culture.

I owe a debt of gratitude to certain store partners who became friends over the span of many years and who shared their coffee knowledge, compassion, and genuine enthusiasm to connect over coffee. Thank you (in no particular order) Sarah Abraham, Aaron Pearlman, Dave Flippen, Amylla Murray, Taigan Reynolds, Jenn McPoland, Jocelyn Stewart, Jesse Fish, Dylan Austin, Cameron Kimmel-Spivey, Brittney Cavender, Taylor Stockett, Kerri La Pratt, Jess Fried, Rachel Piecuch, Jayde Hartman, Gypsy, Jonathan Cole, Jenn Neil, Kirsten Marie Barber, Meggan Peterschick and many more.

Thank you to my editor Patricia D. Eddy, and cover designer Sandy Nelson.

Thank you to Valerie Overton for many words of encouragement and enormous help with edits and content suggestions.

Cast of Primary Characters

- Cliff Burrows – When this book went to press, the Starbucks website listed his title and position as follows: "As group president, Americas, Europe, Middle East and Africa (EMEA) and Teavana, Cliff Burrows is responsible for all of Starbucks operations in the United States, Canada, Latin America, Europe, Russia and the Middle East, as well as the expansion of Teavana retail stores." In the book, I often refer to him as *President of Just About Everything Starbucks*.

- Howard Schultz – The CEO of Starbucks Coffee Company.

- Mallory – A Starbucks headquarters PR person

- Minori Okada – A passionate Starbucks fan from Kyoto, Japan.

- Rose – A friend of mine, whom I've known for more than twenty years. She's been a shareholder since the IPO.

- Andrew Fried – A regional Starbucks president.

- Sessily – A Starbucks store partner and shift supervisor.

- Callie – A developmentally delayed employee at my workplace.

Locations

- Starbucks headquarters – This the Starbucks Support Center, and is often called the "SSC" – 2401 Utah Avenue South. This is in the SODO neighborhood of Seattle, an industrial neighborhood that was once "South of the Dome." We Seattleites blew up the King Dome, and built two sports stadiums in its place. The Starbucks headquarters is less than two miles from my office.
- The First Starbucks – 1912 Pike Place – This is the historic Starbucks in Seattle's Pike Place Market.
- The 1st and Pike Starbucks – A newer Starbucks that opened in 2009.
- Smith Tower Starbucks – Corner of 2nd and Yesler in Seattle. (Now closed.)
- 4th and Cherry Starbucks – This is Starbucks store #101, and has been around since the 1980s. It's also close to my office.
- 15th Avenue Coffee and Tea Starbucks – Once upon a time, it was an "Inspired By" Starbucks with unique food items. In this book, this store will always be referred to as 15th Avenue Coffee and Tea because it was such a concept location during most of the time period the book covers. Now, it's a regular Starbucks, located at 328 – 15th Avenue East, in Seattle.
- My office – 4th and Yesler.
- Pike Place Market – This is a historic area of Seattle with shops, beautiful views, and many tourists. Pike Place Market will often be referred to as "The Market" in this book.
- Eureka, California Starbucks – A Starbucks where Sessily once worked.
- Silverdale Starbucks – A Starbucks where Sessily transferred to

in 2013.

- Roy Street Coffee and Tea – 700 Broadway East, Seattle, WA 98102 – This is an "Inspired By Starbucks" store, meaning that it offers Starbucks whole bean coffees but has a design, food, and atmosphere that don't look at all like a Starbucks. The baristas don't have green aprons, and the food is locally sourced.

Chapter One: The First Time I Met Howard Schultz

April Fool's Day 2008

I didn't think about it being April's Fool's Day. I wasn't expecting any pranks, jokes, or surprises. It was an ordinary work day for me. I was enamored with downtown Seattle, having taken a public defense position in late 2006 in Seattle's Pioneer Square neighborhood, which is a very short hop, skip, and a jump from the retail core of downtown Seattle.

I decided to go to Pike Place Market for lunch. It certainly wasn't going to be anything fancy. What I really wanted was Seattle's famous Beecher's Mac and Cheese. Beecher's is a small business that began in Seattle's Pike Place Market and they make their own amazing cheese. You can buy sandwiches, blocks of cheese, soups, and two varieties of mac and cheese for a quick on-the-go lunch. I didn't have a lot of time, but I was craving mac and cheese, so I headed to the Market.

The quickest route from my office to Beecher's was to enter Seattle's bus tunnel and go from the Pioneer Station to the Westlake Station. Once out of the Westlake Station, you're on Pine Street, which runs parallel to Pike Street, both leading straight to the famous Pike Place Market, known for fish throwers, a farmers market of fruits, veggies and fresh flowers, Beecher's, the Confectional (a store specializing in delicious mini-sized cheesecakes), and the original Starbucks store.

The sun was out. I was thinking about that mac and cheese. I picked up a little speed as I rushed to Beecher's. By the time I reached Pine and Pike Place, I was nearly jogging. My thoughts were stuck on lovely food, and "mac and cheese" repeated in my head like a broken record.

I turned right onto Pike Place from Pine, heading north, only a few feet away from the entrance to Beecher's. "Mac and cheese! Mac and cheese!" I daydreamed about lunch.

Suddenly, I came to a screeching halt. There was a tall gentleman with a small crowd around him blocking my way into Beecher's. My gut told me that this whole group was together. I took a step back and surveyed the situation. The realization hit me. That's Howard Schultz! I stopped and soaked up what was happening around me.

Howard Schultz had been all over the news lately. In January 2008, he returned to the position of CEO of Starbucks, a position he'd stepped down from in the early months of 2000. I realized that there was some sort of event going on. Wherever Howard walked, a circle of people trailed right behind him. An ABC newsman, Terry Moran, held a microphone and asked questions as Howard strolled at a very leisurely pace along Pike Place. I wanted to get a little closer and hear what they were saying.

Mac and cheese was long forgotten.

Howard walked a few feet up Pine Street with Terry next to him, and the small crowd encircling him. Howard was completely unaware of me. He'd never met me before. I stayed back at a distance, straining to hear the conversation between Terry Moran and Howard. I wasn't close enough to catch everything that was being said, but I couldn't risk approaching any closer.

Terry Moran asked Howard whether Starbucks would ever see a return to the historic Starbucks of the 1990s, with large bins of beans and long before warmed breakfast sandwiches. Howard clearly said, "We can never go back to those halcyon days of the 1990s."

Halycon. I blanked out on the meaning of the word. Of course, I knew its meaning, but in that moment, it escaped me. *My God. Howard has a really big vocabulary*, I thought. I made a mental note to look up the word when I got back to my office. As a lawyer by profession, I thought of myself as a wordsmith.

At some point, mid-way between the intersection of Pine Street and Pike Place and the original Starbucks at 1912 Pike Place, the interview came to a natural end. The small crowd of people seemed to thin out a bit, and Howard headed back towards 1912 Pike Place. I must have caught the tail end of this news interview. Howard's back was to me and he opened the door to the original Starbucks. Now was my chance. I could introduce myself.

"Hey! Howard!" I yelled. I was loud. I definitely caught his attention. Now what? I had pretty much yanked on Superman's cape. He was staring right at me, probably wondering why I had yelled his name. I had nothing planned. I was completely unprepared with any words.

Even though I began to sweat a little, I still thought it was pretty cool to meet the CEO of Starbucks. I wracked my brain for something – anything I could use to fill in the growing awkward silence between us. He stood patiently for a solid ten seconds while my mouth was half open but silent. The ten seconds felt like five minutes. I remembered hearing news about Starbucks' new "Mastrena" machines during the March Annual Meeting of Shareholders. Out of my mouth, in a sloppy mumble of words, I asked Howard Schultz some dumb question about when all the Starbucks stores would have the Mastrena espresso machines in them. I'm not sure I even told him my name.

You never get a second chance to make a first impression, and I was pretty sure that I'd screwed that one up in one rapid, tongue-tied moment.

And for me, I headed back down to Beecher's for some mac and cheese.

In 2008, the closest Starbucks to my office was the Smith Tower location. Much has changed since then, and that Smith Tower store closed its doors permanently in 2012. It was an important Starbucks to me. From the time I started working downtown in late 2006 until the store closed, it was a place where partners (Starbucks calls their employees "partners") had welcomed me and invited me to try coffees with them to really immerse myself in the Starbucks experience.

As I sat at Beecher's, I pulled out my phone and called the Smith Tower Starbucks. I knew there was one barista there who would be entertained by my story of this chance meeting with Howard Schultz on April Fool's Day.

I managed to get Collin Longacre, the store manager, on the phone and told him my story.

"I'm so jealous Melody! Lucky you to have that moment with Howard!" I told Collin my worry that I had embarrassed myself when introducing myself to Howard. Collin reassured me. "Don't worry one bit. Howard's probably seen a little bit of *everything* in reaction to him. And Melody, you know there's a big Starbucks event going on at Pike Place Market on April 8th? Would you like to go together?"

"Of course, I'd love to go. I'd have to meet you after work."

"Perfect. It's at six. I'm off in time. Meet you at the store and we'll walk to the Market."

I sat at the counter seating at Beecher's, pushing around my mac and cheese with a fork, having hung up the phone with Collin. I wasn't as hungry as I thought I was. As I played with my food, I had racing thoughts of how strange today's events had turned out to be. And now I was planning to go to an event where Howard would be one week from now. I wondered if I'd get that second chance to make a first impression.

Don't be afraid to tug on Superman's cape.

Chapter Two: Pike Place Roast Day

On April 8, 2008, Starbucks introduced a new coffee blend to their lineup. This blend had been a top secret "Consistent Brew" project, where Starbucks coffee masters experimented with a number of coffees to come up with a perfect *every day* cup of coffee. The idea behind Pike Place Roast coffee was that it would be a consistent cup of coffee that could be found in all Starbucks, at all times.

One lesson that Starbucks learned over the years was that the various flavor profiles found in their coffee offerings could be off-putting to some customers. Those who love coffee know that "*flavor is a geography.*" In fact, that had been a Starbucks motto for close to two decades. Generally speaking, a Starbucks coffee master knows that where a coffee is grown and how it is processed have a dramatic effect on the natural flavors of the coffee. Just as crops and types of apples can taste very different from season to season, depending on the varietal and the weather, coffee too is a farm product. Coffees grown in African countries are often known for fruity or berry flavor notes. This is partly due to the fact that many African coffees are sun dried on tarps with the coffee beans still enveloped in the coffee cherries. Coffees that come from Indonesian countries like Sumatra and Papua New Guinea are characterized by very bold flavors which may occasionally be described as savory and earthy. Latin American coffee growing regions produce a number of coffees with slighter lighter flavor notes and are often known for nutty or cocoa flavors, and high acidity. In Latin America, many coffee farms use a "washed" processing method of handling the coffee cherry which contributes to this distinctive flavor. The coffee bean is cleaned from the cherry and its mucilage by a full immersion in water. I've over simplified a lot of coffee information, but the bottom line is that coffee can vary a lot in flavor from region to region and varietal to varietal.

For Starbucks customers, especially those who are unaware of the unique ways growing regions affect flavors, this ever-rotating coffee flavor profile was often an unsettling surprise. A customer who loved a very bold blend being offered and enjoyed the earthy notes of one coffee might the next week discover that his or her cup of coffee had a grapefruit or citrusy bite to it.

This resulted in some customers thinking, *Starbucks is messing with my coffee*, rather than understanding that different coffees really do have different flavor characteristics. To solve this problem, Starbucks decided to come up with one single blend that would be offered in their stores all day, every day.

The coffee masters went to work, and came up with a light to medium bodied coffee with distinctly Latin American flavor notes. Starbucks called it "Pike Place Roast" in celebration of the place where Starbucks was born: Pike Place Market.

The big launch day was Tuesday, April 8, 2008. Partners got special promotional black t-shirts that said things like "fresh" and "smooth" on the front of them and "Every day. Pike Place Roast" on the back. Across the country, more than 7,000 Starbucks partners wore the promotional Pike Place Roast shirts, cheerfully sampling the new coffee. The sleeve of these shirts used a special brown Starbucks logo, a little more modest than the original logo. The original 1971-version of the Starbucks logo had exposed nipples and an obvious belly button. This 2008 logo designed for the launch of Pike Place Roast, inspired by the original, managed to hide the Siren's nipples with her flowing long hair.

And so Pike Place Roast Day featured an all new, everyday coffee, and an army of Starbucks partners in "bold," "fresh," or "smooth" black t-shirts.

The festivities began in New York City's Bryant Park, with Howard Schultz raving about the new every day brew, while an April New York City wind chill off the Hudson River made a hot cup of coffee a welcome sight. Howard stood before a life-sized mock original 1912 Pike Place Starbucks. News photos of Howard Schultz showed his award winning smile, proudly holding a cup of coffee. In some of the photos he looked a bit like he was shivering.

After the New York event, Howard hopped on a plane and flew to Seattle for the evening festivities: a second kickoff event at Seattle's Pike Place Market.

I worked during the day, oblivious to what was happening in New York City. At that point, all I knew was that there was an evening event surrounding this new blend, and I wanted to go with the Smith Tower store manager, Collin. The evening event was planned late enough that I could leave work at five and hurry to the Market.

I ran over to the Smith Tower and caught up with Collin, who was closing up the store for the day. Together we walked from Seattle's Pioneer Square neighborhood to the Market.

The sight of green aprons and people in Pike Place Roast promotional t-shirts that said "fresh" and "smooth" and more was a tip off that there were lots of partners at this event. Several tables were set up with baristas giving out free sample-sized quarter pound bags of Pike Place Roast to introduce the world to the new coffee blend.

A stage stood proudly on the nineteenth century era red brick road in front of 1912 Pike Place. A band played live music. A district manager got on the stage and spoke first. A few people from the corporate head-quarters spoke as well, but at that time I didn't know who they were. Nonetheless, I listened intently as they rallied around the new coffee blend.

Howard Schultz took the stage too. He talked about the company's "love and passion for coffee" and how Starbucks balances profitability with social responsibility. He was a powerful speaker and I was swayed by his passion and his devotion to all-new blend, Pike Place Roast.

Then-City of Seattle Mayor Greg Nickels got on the stage, made a short speech, and presented Howard with a certificate. April 8, 2008 was officially declared "Pike Place Roast Day" in Seattle. Howard spoke for a few more minutes and then headed off the stage into the Pike Place Starbucks, that first store where it all began.

Collin and I stood in the area between the stage and the door to the 1912 Pike Place Starbucks, meaning that in order for Howard to go in-side the store, he had to pass right by us. There was quite a crowd in all directions around the stage, and as soon as Howard stepped down from the stage, he was swamped. It was an incredible sight. He slowly made his way to the door of Pike Place Starbucks, walking backwards almost in slow motion. He was literally taking backward baby steps, attempt-ing to shake as many hands, and greet as many fans as possible before entering the store. This must be an everyday experience in the life of a celebrity.

A curious thing happened. As Howard walked in slow motion, numer-ous hands pulled cards from wallets, and pushed Starbucks cards in his direction, hoping to capture a moment of his time. The dance repeated over and over again. Howard would accept a card, stand still for a moment to autograph it, and hand it back. Before long, I realized that most of the cards were distinctive "Starbucks partner cards." Those cards identify Starbucks employees by name, and employee number. They're sent to new partners shortly after starting employment with Starbucks.

Howard Schultz was swarmed[1]. The thought that occurred to me at that moment was simply, "Wow, Howard Schultz could use a little security around him." Collin from the Smith Tower store got his silver partner card signed. Howard continued in this delicate feat of walking backward to 1912 Pike Place, while slowly signing cards and being pounced on and lunged at by a crowd of customers and partners, all huge fans of Starbucks.

I pulled out my Starbucks registered card and passed it to him to sign at the right moment. I was a full arm's length away from him and passed the card gingerly over the heads of others. It helps to be a tall person. He quickly scribbled his name on it with a Sharpie pen and as he looked

---

1   Almost six years after this event, I realized that "swarmed" is precisely the right word. One rainy, Saturday morning in January 2014, I went to the University Village 3 Starbucks, and sat down for a minute with a latte. I had just sat down and a partner whom I really like came up to me and said, "Melody, I got five minutes left of this break? Can I sit with you?" We had an enormous amount of conversation in five minutes. We got on the topic of 'the first time you ever met Howard Schultz' because Howard had been in the University Village 3 Starbucks one day before. The partner said to me, "I met Howard Schultz at this event in April 2008, at the Pike Place Market, and he signed my partner card!" and then he described in detail, and exactly as I had remembered it too, "You should have seen it. Howard got off the stage and got swarmed! I handed him my partner card to sign and tried to shake his hand too!"

back up, he made eye contact with me. Howard passed the now-autographed Pike Place card back to me and said, "Oh, I remember you from last week."

I had a good feeling. The crowd's energy was fueled by the passion for a new blend, like a sport's team victory parade.

On the day Pike Place Roast was official born, once again Howard disappeared into 1912 Pike Place Starbucks.

Make history with your innovation.

Chapter Three: Thanksgiving Blend

The "Thanksgiving Blend event" was a one-of-a-kind coffee tasting inside the Starbucks headquarters, and by some incredible luck, in early November 2008, I received an email (from someone I didn't know) for this "First Ever Gold Card Event". I probably should have bought a lottery ticket the day I received my invitation. At a minimum, my recently registered Starbucks card was really delivering amazing rewards.

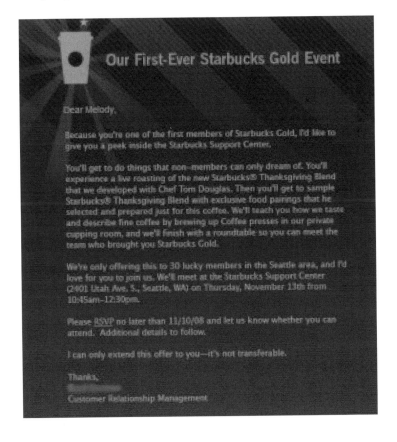

Dear Melody, because you're one of the first members of Starbucks Gold, I'd like to give you a peek inside the Starbucks Support Center...

The email invited me to go to an exclusive event with no more than thirty customers to *experience a live roasting of the new Starbucks Thanksgiving Blend ... developed with Chef Tom Douglas.* The event was scheduled for Thursday November 13, 2008 from 10:45 to 12:30. I couldn't RSVP and arrange time off from work fast enough.

I was a little anxious. I had never been to a roasting event and I didn't know what it was.[2] A few hours before the event started, in a moment of silliness, I even emailed the contact person and asked if it was okay to wear jeans. She replied back to me, "Sure! Wear whatever you'd like- and enjoy it all!"

I arrived on time and checked in with a front desk receptionist at the Starbucks headquarters. Soon I was joined by a group of customers and a few Starbucks marketing and PR people. There were only about fifteen customers in attendance. We went into a large main auditorium with a small coffee roaster illuminated by skylights. This auditorium, I later learned, is the site of many large Starbucks corporate events, with Howard Schultz and other members of the leadership team. In addition, it's the site of monthly coffee roasting events.

There were Starbucks coffee masters around the coffee roaster, crafting a small batch of no more than fifteen pounds[3] of Starbucks Thanksgiving Blend before my very eyes. They carefully loaded green beans into the roaster's hopper, monitoring the roasting process. Along the way,

---

2   Though this was my first roasting event, I went to a couple others in the years to come. They all have a magical quality to them.

3   This roaster inside the headquarters is small. The coffee roasters at the large Starbucks roasting facilities in places like Kent, Washington can roast 300 to 900 pound batches of coffee.

the coffee masters retrieved tiny samples of the coffee from the roaster, monitoring the transition from green to cinnamon roast to the beautiful dark roast Thanksgiving Blend. They stood by, on alert, awaiting the tell-tale noise of coffee beans as they *pop*. It was the first time I ever saw coffee being roasted.

Chef Tom Douglas stood at the microphone addressing a crowd as the auditorium slowly filled with corporate partners who left their desks, offices, and cubicles to join in the ritual of a fresh coffee roasting event.

Tom Douglas told stories of how Thanksgiving Blend coffee was developed and his long history with Starbucks. He told stories of old, going back to the late 1970s, when Starbucks delivered coffee regularly to his restaurants in a van, and Starbucks employees would barge into his kitchens, checking the timers on his brewed coffee and badger his chefs until they swore they were serving only fresh-brewed coffee to their patrons. As Tom spoke, he made a motion as if he were swatting away flies referring to the Starbucks intruders in his kitchen.

To develop Thanksgiving Blend coffee, the Starbucks coffee team started hunting for the right blend of beans long before Thanksgiving. Tom Douglas was cooking up turkey dinners with Starbucks coffee masters and tasting various blends of coffee with turkey, gravy, stuffing, potatoes, pumpkin pie and a full Thanksgiving meal–all during a hot July!

Howard Schultz spoke too. He waxed nostalgic about the enduring partnership between Starbucks and Tom Douglas and his pride to be the sole source of coffee in the fine Tom Douglas restaurants. Howard was right: Tom Douglas restaurants are amazing places to eat, and a local favorite for many. To this day, Dahlia Bakery, Tanaka San, The Palace Kitchen and Lola are places that you might find me now and then. Dahlia Bakery is an alcove of a space adjacent to the Dahlia Lounge restaurant, and a perfect grab-and-go spot for a cup of Tom's famous tomato soup, muffins, cookies, and other baked goodies that Tom Douglas is known for.

When the coffee was ready to come out of the roaster, the presentations stopped mid-sentence and monitors turned to the equipment. A microphone next to the oven amplified the sound of popping coffee beans. Next thing I knew, freshly roasted coffee beans poured into a cooling tray below. It was magical. The aroma of freshly roasted coffee filled the room.

After the roasting event, the small group of Gold Card customers, a few folks from the Starbucks card department, and a few select Starbucks partners all walked up to the cupping room on the eighth floor of the headquarters. Many people don't realize that a cupping of coffee is not quite the same thing as a traditional tasting of coffee inside a Starbucks store. A wise coffee master once told me that to learn about coffee, you have to "taste and compare, taste and compare." Learning about coffee requires tasting coffees side by side so you have a basis of comparison. The cupping method of tasting coffee is what professional roasters do to ensure quality coffee production. It is not coffee brewed in a French press. Small cups have fine grounds in them, hot water is poured directly on the grounds, and then the coffee brews for about four minutes. After the brewing time, a crust forms atop the coffee which is broken, releasing the aroma, and then scraped off. The coffee is ready for tasting by slurping up the coffee from a spoon.

We cupped Guatemala Antigua coffee, Sumatra, and the Thanksgiving Blend. We were a group of amateur coffee slurpers, but there were a lot of smiles in the room, as it was a new experience for all the customers.

Howard Schultz joined us in the cupping room, thanked us all for being there, and talked about how we were all selected as loyal customers. He didn't call us out and speak to us individually, but there was a moment when I was sure he recognized me in the group.

It didn't end there. After the cupping, our group of fifteen customers was escorted into a large meeting room. We sat around a large conference table with gift bags waiting for each of us. Around the perimeter of the room, chairs were set up for Starbucks corporate employees from various departments. Our event host asked us questions about our Starbucks experiences, about using the card, and what we thought of the gold card. We talked freely. The Starbucks employees took notes as we spoke.

This was an "ah ha" moment for me. Customers had come from all over Western Washington for the event. Nearly every customer had a favorite store and a firm Starbucks ritual. Every customer in the group was passionate about Starbucks. They loved having their gold card and they loved their Starbucks experiences. Every customer was a daily, if not more frequent, customer.

The epiphany moment was not that Starbucks employees were listening to us, rather it was that I realized I was not alone. I was humbled to be in this group. I realized that there were lots of people who passionately enjoyed Starbucks. I realized that I never wanted to be called "Starbucks' biggest fan." People have said that about me a couple of times but it can't be true. I am *not* Starbucks' biggest fan. Lots of customers have a powerful connection with Starbucks. Through my blog, I've only managed to become a *visible* fan. In 2008, I was a little more visible than the average customer because of my participation on MyStarbucksIdea.com, but being visible does not mean that one is the "biggest fan."

Still to this day, I think back to the group of fifteen people who humbled me and my own interest in Starbucks. Now when people say things to me like, "you must be Starbucks' biggest fan" I always firmly say, "no," and think back to that Thanksgiving Blend event.

When people say corny things about Starbucks being "bigger than coffee," or when Starbucks employees say, "We're in the people business, serving coffee," I know they're right. Many people from all over think of themselves as "Starbucks' biggest fan."

I walked out of the Thanksgiving Blend event feeling like my world had been set on fire–I was high on coffee–and I got to see something unique and special that most customers (and even some Starbucks partners) never get to enjoy. I wanted to share my passion for Starbucks, but at that point I didn't have a blog, so I continued using any other online resource that I had, including MyStarbucksIdea.com. That was the first time I thought I might have my own blog about Starbucks someday.

I walked out of the Starbucks Support Center (the headquarters) an inspired Starbucks customer and thankful for any opportunity for these unique one-of-a-kind experiences. It was one year later that I launched StarbucksMelody.com, but that's another story that we'll get to.

Set your fans on fire – give them a chance to experience something rare.

Chapter Four: 15ᵗʰ Avenue Coffee and Tea

S ummers in Seattle are filled with long days of near perfect weather. In 2009, Starbucks experimented with a new concept store which opened July 24ᵗʰ of that year: "15ᵗʰ Avenue Coffee and Tea."

The Starbucks in that location closed one day and a tall wood fence sprang up around it. Signs read: "Your neighborhood coffee shop is getting a makeover."

Word got out that this new store would look and feel like a small neighborhood coffee shop, not a Starbucks. *The Seattle Times'* Coffee City Blog (written by Melissa Allison) reported on this "undercover Starbucks" on July 16, 2009.[4] They spoke of its "rustic, eco-friendly style". Now and then, I even heard people calling this store a "sleuth Starbucks."

There were many ways that this store was unlike any other Starbucks. It had a manual espresso machine, it offered beer and wine, and unique local foods. The store's new name and the fact that beer and wine were on the menu created buzz and some controversy too.[5]

---

4   http://seattletimes.com/html/coffeecity/2009482990_coming_soon_an_undercover_star.html

5   http://usatoday30.usatoday.com/money/industries/food/2009-07-16-starbucks-new-concept_n.htm

Today, there are a number of Starbucks stores that offer beer and wine, but this store on 15th East was the trendsetting, experimental store. A Starbucks that serves beer and wine is now called an Evenings Starbucks. As I write this, Seattle has four of them.

I remember opening day well. I was brutally tired. One of my work obligations on occasion is to carry a DUI beeper. This means that if a person arrested for Driving Under the Influence wishes to talk to an attorney at two in the morning, my phone rings and I take the call. I provide legal advice and then go back to sleep. It's not an onerous extra duty, but it does mean that my sleep will be completely disrupted by calls in the wee hours of the morning.

I arrived at 15th Avenue Coffee and Tea early on opening day. I wanted to be the first person in the door. It must've been five in the morning. This was painful after having been on the phone three hours earlier with a DUI call. I was tired as could be. I really did need some coffee.

Despite the hour, several people were already lined up at the entrance when I arrived. I managed to be customer number two in the door on that grand opening day.

Along one wall, there were deep metal coffee bins framed in wood. Each had a nametag for a specific coffee. The tags looked like oversized garden tags, but instead of tomatoes and carrots, the tags held famous Starbucks coffee names like Verona and Italian Roast. More than a year later, a partner mentioned to me in passing that those bins took their design and placement inspiration from a British coffee house called Monmouth Coffee. I liked the metal coffee bins because they vaguely reminded me of the days in the 1990s when Starbucks partners scooped freshly-roasted coffee from labeled drawers and weighed out the amount of coffee you wanted to take home with you.

The pastries at 15th Avenue Coffee and Tea came from a local Seattle business called Essential Baking Company and the donuts were from another Seattle business: Mighty-O donuts. Later, the store added some little quiches and other food items. When Seattle's weather turned cold in late autumn, the store served a Tom Douglas tomato soup, which I thoroughly enjoyed.

On opening morning, I took a chair in a far corner of the store. I wanted to fall asleep but I was still taking in the rich design of reclaimed wood and hanging lights that were styled reminiscent of the lights at the first Starbucks at 1912 Pike Place.

I opened up my laptop and furiously sent tweets that I was inside the new concept store. As I sipped coffee, I recognized a few faces of Starbucks corporate partners checking the place out, giving it their nod of approval.

I scanned Twitter and a few other websites to check out what was being said about the new store.

Arthur Rubinfeld, a Starbucks executive in charge of global store growth, approached me and said a polite hello. He made a comment that the view of the store from my seat was particularly great. "You picked the best seat in the house." I agreed. I wasn't in a social mood and really wanted to be ignored. I was dead tired from the night's string of DUI calls. I know Arthur and I spoke for several minutes, but I barely recall the conversation. I left the store that morning brimming with excitement (and exhaustion), and headed into the office.

It wasn't long before I was back. Two or three days later, I returned to 15th Avenue Coffee and Tea with my friend Jodie. It was early evening and I wanted to check out the store's nighttime vibe, when beer and wine were being served. We sat there talking and in walked Howard Schultz. The store had only been open a few days, and Howard looked like he was doing the same thing: checking out the evening ambiance.

I asked Howard if he would autograph a couple of Starbucks cards for me. A flash of surprise passed over his face as surely he wondered at how many Starbucks cards he would ultimately end up signing for me. Little did he know, I had used the Starbucks card he'd previously signed on Pike Place Roast Day so much that his autograph had almost worn off and the card showed signs of the wear and tear. That old card was now faded, beginning to crack, and with only a large blue "H" in his cursive on it.

Howard said "sure" without any hesitation. I pulled two cards out of my wallet and asked a barista for a Sharpie pen. Finding a Sharpie in any Starbucks is never a difficult task. He signed both cards.

"What do you think of the store, Melody?" Howard asked. He seemed genuinely interested in knowing my response. Howard was relaxed and talkative. [6]

After a brief moment of hesitation, I told him I loved it. I paused before answering, wondering if I should tell him that I was puzzled at the store's lack of comfy seating.

That conversation wasn't a long one, but to this day it remains one of my favorites. He wasn't wearing that look of 'I'm *in a rush*' and didn't appear to have numerous other demands dividing his attention.

A few days after Howard signed my Starbucks cards, I took one of them to a local frame shop in Belltown: Seattle Custom Framing. If I didn't frame it, the autograph would again wear off. I'd already pressed my luck by getting cards signed by Howard on two separate occasions. That second special Pike Place Starbucks card, signed by Howard in July

---

6   After a number of interactions with Howard, I slowly began to figure out the difference between Howard's "I'm busy" face and his "You can talk now" face but at this point in time, I hadn't finessed this yet. However, I had caught him at a good time on this particular evening.

2009, hangs in my office to this day.

Eventually, I tossed out that old, cracked and worn Starbucks card, which only had Howard's faded blue Sharpie ink letter "H" on it. It was a hard thing to do. How often do you get a piece of Starbucks history – Pike Place Roast Day – and Howard's autograph all in one day?

15th Avenue Coffee and Tea quickly became one of my favorite places to go have coffee, breakfast, or Tom Douglas' tomato soup. The store went through a lot of changes over the years to come and later Starbucks opened up another Seattle concept store called Roy Street, but for several years, this store remained one of my favorite places to hang out, relax, have coffee, and talk to the store's partners.

During the first two years it was open, 15th Avenue Coffee and Tea offered regular coffee tastings, cuppings and tea tastings. It was unique in the intensity of its coffee education and I learned a lot about coffee from that store.

One particular bit of education sticks in my mind. A barista who had seen me talking to Howard gave me a stern warning. "Melody, never call him Howie." I had no idea. I hadn't thought of doing so and I definitely don't know him well enough to use a nickname. Well, let's be honest. I barely know Howard. He barely knows me. She repeated her warning: "Melody, he hates the name Howie." Okay, I got it. *Thank you for the warning*, I thought. It was a mistake I never made and a train wreck averted unlike the moment when I yanked on his cape at the Market.

There is one more anecdote I want to share about 15th Avenue Coffee and Tea. This store was the first place I met Andrew Fried. When I met him, he was a Regional Vice President at Starbucks, meaning he was in charge of hundreds of Starbucks stores in Washington, Oregon, Alaska, and the Northern edge of California.[7] Given the large swath of Starbucks

---

7   He left the Seattle area and was promoted to an executive in an

stores under his watchful eye, in this flagship hometown region, he has a leadership role at Starbucks. I was quick to melt at his blue eyes and southern drawl, giving away the fact that he wasn't a Washington native. One evening in July, a Starbucks barista at 15th Avenue Coffee and Tea introduced us. We got the chance to talk, and I told him that professionally, I'm a public defense attorney. When I tell some Starbucks partners that I'm a public defense lawyer and attempt to explain what it means to represent those who otherwise wouldn't be able to afford an attorney, their eyes glaze over. It's as if the only conversation they want to have is about Starbucks.

Andrew engaged me with a genuine interest, telling me that at one point, early in his career he'd seriously considered becoming a lawyer. He'd wanted a career in politics, law, and public policy. I was sure, if we had the chance to sit down over a French press and kill an hour's worth of time, we'd have some good conversations.

Sometimes the oddest places can bring people together.

---

international Starbucks market, but I'll get to that later.

Chapter Five: How StarbucksMelody.com Was Born

On a regular basis, I am asked, "Melody, how did you end up with a Starbucks blog?" The blog known as StarbucksMelody.com was born on September 9, 2009. The entire experience has been learning by doing. I can say without a doubt, it was all trial by fire.

The spark of the idea began in 2008. I started to think that I had enough to say about Starbucks that I could write about them in a blog. I had no idea how to create a blog, though. I simply didn't have the technical skills, and to be honest, I didn't want to pour hours into learning HTML. Not to mention there already were a couple of popular blogs about Starbucks. Mine certainly would *not* be the first. It was unlikely to ever be the largest. And it wouldn't be the last. But it would be mine.

In the autumn of 2009, I was reading another online website about Starbucks, and buried in the comments I saw that Starbucks was testing a product called the "Honey Vanilla Vivanno." The comment said that the Honey Vanilla Vivanno was being test marketed in Sacramento.

The Vivanno was a smoothie. You put a banana, milk, ice, and a few other things into the blender, and you end up with a smoothie. When Starbucks introduced smoothies into their lineup, they decided to give them their own unique name: the Vivanno. However, it was really just a smoothie with a Starbuckian name.

In a rash move, I decided was going to try it. Why was it a rash move?

Because Seattle is more than seven hundred miles from Sacramento. I decided to drive to Sacramento and back over Labor Day Weekend. I think I spent more hours in the car than out of it over those three days. I made the eleven hour drive with only one stop in Oregon for a night's rest. I didn't know the city of Sacramento, and I had no idea if the Honey Vanilla Vivanno was at some stores or all of them, but I got off Interstate 5 at a random Sacramento exit. I drove around until I found a Starbucks downtown. As ubiquitous as Starbucks has become, it wasn't that hard to find a Starbucks store. Sure enough, they had the Honey Vanilla Vivanno. I tried it. I loved it! It had a tangy vanilla yogurt flavor with lots of honey drizzle on top. There was a second fruity Vivanno Blend but after one Vivanno I was too full to try a second one. I snuck two small pictures with my old camera phone. I didn't own a smart phone.

Powered by this special test version Starbucks smoothie and a lot of daydreaming about my future Starbucks blog, I got back into my 1993 Acura Integra and headed north. I had my first blog article: The Honey Vanilla Vivanno. Unfortunately, I still didn't have a blog to post it on.

Labor Day weekend ended, and as luck would have it, I didn't return immediately to work. Months before, I had been summoned to Jury Duty in King County Superior Court for the week after Labor Day. As a practicing attorney, I always get a little excited about jury duty. It's great fun to see trials in action, and even watching the *voir dire* process (also known as jury selection, when attorneys question prospective jurors) is entertaining. The day after Labor Day, I waited in a big room on the first floor of King County Superior Court. Fingers crossed. I wanted to be on a jury, or at least experience an interesting *voir dire*.

Lucky for me, I did. The court staff called out nearly one hundred numbers for a jury pool on one case. I was number seventy-seven. A large segment of the jury waiting room emptied out in one fell swoop. That's a lot of prospective jurors for one case. Usually this means either this was going to be a high visibility trial where finding impartial jurors would be a problem or that the trial would be excessively long and it would be difficult to find jurors who could spend weeks serving on a jury.

The first twelve people seated in a jury box are called the "presumptive jury," but as people get bumped off the jury for one reason or another, other people with higher numbers take their place. In King County, thirteen people are chosen for a jury in Superior Court: 12 jury members and one alternate. All of them must pay attention, and no one knows who the alternate is.

After a lot of waiting, the bailiff escorted us into the courtroom. The questioning began. "Has anyone heard of a case where a City of Seattle Firefighter fell down a pole shaft?" A number of people *had* heard of the case. This was expected to be a long trial, lasting for weeks, hearing evidence regarding an injured firefighter. The injuries were totally debilitating. There were lots of questions about damages. It was clear that the plaintiff would be seeking large monetary damages for the city of Seattle's alleged negligence.

During the downtime, I used my old cell phone to follow my twitter stream as best as I could. My phone was woefully out of date and it was tough for me to tweet from the phone, but at least I could read my twitter stream to stave off the boredom during some of the less interesting court processes and procedures.

As part of the process, the prospective jury is shuffled in and out of the courtroom several times. There are parts of the court proceedings that you're not privy to as a potential juror. During these times, I made small talk with the people immediately around me.

Juror seventy-five showed telltale signs of social media addiction: neck bent, eyes glued to a tiny glowing screen, the flash of social media icons reflected in her eyes and on the phone's display. Her name was Jenn Wainwright and we soon discovered that we were both on Twitter. We quickly began following each other.

Juror number seventy-six was wedged between Jenn and I, and despite the fact that we must've pestered him a bit, we talked around him. I instantly liked Jenn. My gut said she was a great person. I asked her what she did for a living and she said that she had her own small business making websites for people. I pushed further. "Do you make blogs too?" She said that she did. I had a moment of realization, as clear as could be: this is it. I will have a blog.

To be absolutely sure, I had to ask the right follow up question. What if my gut was wrong and she was one of these types that never steps foot inside Starbucks?

"Nothing gets between me and my Grande Iced Soy Caramel Macchiato," she replied. The stars aligned. Sometimes the universe just puts the right people in your path at the right time.

This civil suit with the firefighter looked like it was going to be a battle of a trial. I spent my entire jury duty on this case's *voir dire*. Many people were released for good cause by the judge: they couldn't be away from work that long, they had a vacation planned soon, and they had kids to take care for.

The numbers dropped off, but Jenn and I remained. We didn't end up on to the jury, but it was close. During that week, we spent our time talking about websites, blogs, and social media. It was day one into the week long jury selection that we struck a deal.

Lunch breaks saw us running up and down the stairs in King County Superior Court to find something quick and nearby. I was trailing behind Jenn, yet still carrying on our conversation. "Hey what do you charge per hour to start a blog?" I asked.

Running down twelve flights of stairs in the 100-year old courthouse with a crowd around us, she yelled at me, "It's twenty-five dollars an hour!"

I didn't think about it. I was merely trying to keep up with her. I yelled back those three words of great legal significance: It's a deal!"

We started immediately. Every jury selection break we talked and planned. We met very early in the remaining mornings of jury selection, and the weekend following jury duty we worked at the University Village Starbucks. StarbucksMelody.com was pounded out in a matter of days.

"What is this blog going to be called? StarbucksFanNews.com? StarbucksInfo?" she asked me.

"I'm Melody and it is my blog about Starbucks. It should be StarbucksMelody.com." It would have the stamp of my personality, even if that meant a little unpredictability to it. What fun would it be without that?

"You've got the hard part, Melody. Most blogs fail because the blog owners stop updating them. You have to update this site regularly," she cautioned me.

I promised myself I would.

I wasn't always sure what I would write about. But I followed a pattern. I wrote an article, published it, and then tweeted about it. That was the recipe that I followed almost indefinitely. I'm still doing that today. I had one more rule: I wrote consistently.

Two months into blogging, my analytics reported that I was getting about thirty unique visitors a day on average. Some days it crept up to seventy five unique visitors. There were times I looked at my blog's analytics and thought that it was reminiscent of a flat-line EKG signal and that it would never go up again.

But it grew. Sometimes two steps forwards and one step back.

Something else big happened in September 2009. When Howard Schultz returned as CEO, he planned a transformation of Starbucks, ushering in a wave of innovation. From Mastrena espresso machines to launching of the crowd-sourcing idea website MyStarbucksIdea.com to the national launch of the Via Ready Brew instant coffee product.

In mid-September 2009, I went to a public gathering and rally for the new Via Ready Brew, held during a lunch hour in the parking lot of the Starbucks headquarters. While there, I was introduced to a Seattle Times reporter: Melissa Allison. I told her about my brand new blog. Much to my surprise, on September 15, 2009, my very first mention in the news appeared: Melissa reported about StarbucksMelody.com in her Coffee City blog.[8] What good luck! I started StarbucksMelody.com with a small bang. There were no fireworks, but I was on my way.

I always liked that Via Ready Brew and StarbucksMelody.com were born in the same month.

And that was how I started my blog. Thank you jury duty.

Never skip your civic duty.

---

8   http://seattletimes.com/html/coffeecity/2009872497_starbucksmelody_arguably_the_c.html

Chapter Six: November 1, 2009

The morning of November 1, 2009, I dropped by 15th Avenue Coffee and Tea Starbucks on my way to work. I had an appointment there with Lincoln, a Seattle Times journalist, who wanted to ask me Starbucks-related questions.

I met with him, talked a bit and showed him the store. At that time, that store had completely unique food offerings, a manual espresso machine, no blenders for Frappuccinos, and a one-of-a-kind for mercantile-looking store design.

Lincoln wanted to get a photo of me outside the store for the article. He walked ahead of me, disappearing out the front door. I was a few feet behind him and I didn't make it out the door, though I was heading in that direction. Howard Schultz walked in. Of course he recognized me and said hello. It had only been a few months since we had run into each other at this very store. He ordered a beverage and waited near the espresso bar pick up area.

He had a look on his face as if to say, "I'm in a hurry to get to work," but I ignored it. I wanted to tell him about my blog.

Howard appeared a little preoccupied, nonetheless he could see that I was eager to have a conversation with him. I was nearly bouncing on my tippy toes, genuinely excited to have started my blog all about Starbucks.

"Howard I launched a blog!" I was very excited about StarbucksMelody.com.

His interest appeared piqued. "What's it called Melody?"

"StarbucksMelody.com!" Right then, his beverage came up and he headed out the door, politely excusing himself.

What have I done? I thought. Suddenly I felt sweaty and nauseous all at once. I'd told the CEO of Starbucks that I'm writing a blog about his company. The weight of that hit me. You can't tell the CEO of a corporation that you're writing about them and then not make it a success. How often does a fan launch a blog and then tell the CEO to his face what she has done? That had been an important thirty second conversation.

The pressure of the moment settled over me. I had to do everything in my power to make StarbucksMelody.com a success. I would spend money on the blog. I would update it faithfully. I would use Twitter and Facebook to market the blog. I would tell my friends about it, and every single barista that I knew. I stood shell shocked for about a minute, only to realize that Lincoln was still waiting for me at the front of the store.

Unfortunately, this episode went from bad to worse. I stepped outside, and saw Lincoln with his camera in hand. "I took some pictures of you two!"

"What?" I was baffled. "You were taking pictures of me talking with Howard?" I asked.

"Yeah. Through the window. That'll be great for a story."

Well, that is what the Seattle Times does. They're a newspaper after all. And Howard Schultz is a public figure – probably every photo of him is newsworthy. I was troubled that my photo could end up in the Seattle Times via pictures taken surreptitiously.

The pressure was on. The Seattle Times mentioned me in a story[9] and

9   http://seattletimes.com/html/businesstechnology/2010171954_starbucks01.html

I had told Howard to his face that I had a blog.

I will not fail.

Truth is stranger than fiction.

Chapter Seven: Introducing Sessily

In March of 2010, I went on a road trip to Eureka, California. My old car still had a few more good road trips in her. True, the electrical was glitchy, and the driver's side window wouldn't roll down, but the engine was still strong. It was impossible for me to use a Starbucks drive-thru, though. I was often lost at the thought of what the "Starbucks Drive Through Experience" might be. But a road trip to Eureka, California was merited.

Sessily, a Starbucks shift supervisor in Eureka, had emailed me some Starbucks chalkboard art. She was responded to a blog article where I put a call out for great chalkboard art. I promised the best one a Starbucks gift card. One of the partners in Sessily's store did amazing artwork and it stood out heads and shoulders above the other responses I'd received.

My intuition told me that Sessily would be someone I liked. I don't know how, but I could tell this in a few, short emails. I used the artwork that Sessily emailed me on the blog, and told her it was some of the best I'd seen for chalkboard art.

Baristas who wear green aprons are superheroes – and sometimes super artistic.

I had arranged for a little vacation time and drove like a mad woman. No breaks, except for gasoline. I had a good feeling about this.

There aren't that many stores in Eureka, California, so getting to the right one wasn't hard at all. I called from my cell phone when I got within an hour of her store – she was there. "Hey, I'm Melody, and I'm coming to visit you! Remember the art work you submitted to my blog?"

She knew who I was. "You're StarbucksMelody?" Little did I know that I'd interrupted her scrubbing a drain in the store, down on her hands and knees.

She bubbled over with excitement. I think bubbling over makes its own special noise – I know it because I'm prone to it myself.

I walked into the small café-only Starbucks in Eureka, still stretching my stiff legs from hours of driving. Sessily recognized me instantly and greeted me with a hug. I knew I had suddenly made a new friend. She reminded me of a beautiful bird. Something about her features reminded me of an elegant peacock, and her hair was adorned with what I later learned were her signature feathers. She was a big personality.

The time slipped by. A few hours felt like a few minutes. After visiting Sessily, I found my way to a hotel and crashed for the night before heading back north to Seattle.

It was a wonderful trip. Well worth it. We kept in touch through emails and Facebook over the many years to come. Three years after this one short trip to Eureka, she moved to a city not far from Seattle. She and I go to Starbucks together, shop for shoes in Seattle's University Village shopping center, and share French presses of coffee.

There are no strangers here, only friends we haven't met.

Chapter Eight: The Via Ready Brew Bearista Bear

Minori Okada, a customer in the Kyoto area of Japan, was incredibly passionate about Starbucks. Through Twitter, email, and StarbucksMelody.com, we'd exchanged emails and messages. Numerous times, Minori had emailed me photos of Starbucks stores in Japan so I could use them on my blog. In my collection of Starbucks cards, one of my all-time favorites is the Kyoto city Starbucks card, which Minori sent to me as a surprise in the mail.

I loved connecting with him. He told me he made regular trips to Seattle to go to the first store at 1912 Pike Place, and he assured me that we'd meet in person someday.

In April 2010, seven months after its introduction in the United States, Starbucks ushered Via Ready Brew into Japan. This product was considered a game changer for Starbucks. Via Ready Brew comes in single-serve packages, ready to make eight perfect ounces of an instant hot coffee.

In Japan, Via Ready Brew was called "Via Coffee Essence" and launched with a lot of emphasis on branded products: cups, mugs, Via carrying cases, Via-branded stir sticks and much more. In particular, the Japan market even got an adorable Via Bearista Bear. It always seemed like Japan got all the cool merchandise.

The Via Bearista Bear was a small, traditional bear, with a cute orange apron that said "Via" on it. In both the U.S. and Japan, orange was part of the marketing theme for Via, and baristas in both countries donned special orange aprons and sampled the new instant coffee. These orange Via aprons were made in classic Starbucks style: two big pockets on the front, ties on the back, and the word Via in white letters against a small brown square centered on the front of the apron.

The United States didn't get that cute little Bearista bear to sell in stores. Via merchandise in Japan vastly outweighed Via merchandise in the United States.

I'd been talking to Minori via Twitter, and he'd tweeted pictures of this cute bear. #Adorbs, I tweeted back. That Via Bearista Bear showed me how Starbucks has the ability to connect fans all over the world. It was the first moment of connection with another Starbucks customer across the Pacific. And I quickly counted him as one of several friends made through a connection over coffee.

Much to my surprise, about a week later, one showed up at my work. Minori wanted me to have one. We'd connected.

Via was a big deal. Howard wrote this about the launch of Via in Japan:

Date: April 12, 2010

Re: A Message from Howard: The Starbucks Growth Story in Asia

Dear Partners,

I'm writing you today from Tokyo, where we are launching Starbucks VIA® in 870 Starbucks stores in Japan. I am joined by other members of the Senior Leadership Team (including John Culver, Arthur Rubinfeld, Annie Young-Scrivner, Vivek Varma and Mary Wagner, our new svp, Global R&D) for this exciting milestone for the company following our successful introduction of Starbucks VIA in the U.S., Canada and the United Kingdom.

In-home coffee consumption in Japan represents a huge opportunity *for Starbucks. We believe Starbucks VIA will offer Japanese customers another fantastic premium coffee option, allowing them to enjoy Starbucks quality coffee in a convenient, single-serve format. Our research shows that 80 percent of our customers regularly drink coffee at home. And in Japan, at-home coffee consumption is a $5 billion market. I was here in Japan two months ago and I could not be more proud of the work the team here has delivered. Our Japanese partners are excited, and when that happens, I know we have a "hit on our hands."*

Via Ready Brew was a hit in Japan. But for me, that little Via Bearista Bear was the hit that I held in my hands. It was my constant reminder that Starbucks brought customers who live a world apart a little closer together. And it reminded me of a friend in Japan.

Doesn't matter if you're in Kyoto or Seattle, the global, universal experience of Starbucks brings people together.

Chapter Nine: Memorial Day Weekend 2010

The first time I met Minori Okada in person was in 2010 over Memorial Day weekend. He was in town to visit the original Starbucks and he wanted to see 15th Avenue Coffee and Tea too. Through Twitter, emails, and a phone call, we arranged to meet in person at the Starbucks store on the corner of First and Pike Street in downtown Seattle. This, by . the way, is not the first store, but rather a newer store a few blocks away from the original Starbucks.

Minori had made several trips to Seattle, though this was the first time I had ever met him. When he arrived, he brought with him a number of Starbucks Japan paper bags, with to/from labels neatly attached. Presents from Japan. On this Memorial Day 2010, he planned to give out presents to many partners he had met when he had visited Starbucks in the winter of 2009, and some partners that he knew from a trip in 2004.

Minori told me that he really wanted to meet Howard. He wanted a chance to shake his hand and tell him in person how much he loved Starbucks. In 2009, when Minori was here, he apparently went to the Starbucks headquarters reception desk and asked to meet Howard Schultz. They prepared a name badge for him, but he never got further than the reception desk. You can't walk in off the street, into the headquarters, and expect to meet Howard Schultz. Probably every minute of Howard's day is planned, and you'd have to be a true VIP to be able to drop in and get to meet up with him. It makes sense that you can't spontaneously drop in on Howard, but it was still a disappointment for Minori.

After months of tweets and emails, it was great to meet Minori in person. When I arrived, he had already nabbed a table. The sight of a friendly Japanese man holding numerous Starbucks Japan paper sacks clued me in that I'd found him. I knew right away those paper bags were presents. I would do the same thing if I was planning Starbucks gift giving. By the time we met at the First and Pike Starbucks, he'd already been to the 1912 Pike Place Starbucks. I ordered my latte, and as I drank it, we plotted our day of Starbucks touristing. He wanted to do the exact same things that I did. "Let's go visit Starbucks stores," I said and he was on the same wavelength.

There are only a few people who can have an entire day of "Starbucks Geeking Out" quite like I can. I'm happy to meet those who can withstand this level of Starbucks overdosing. With friends like Sessily and Minori, I think I've met my match at last.

On Minori's previous trip to Seattle in 2009, the First and Pike had had a different store manager than the one managing it in 2010. That previous store manager, Lisa, is still to this day a mega talent and absolutely sweet to connect with. Unfortunately for the store, but fortunately for Starbucks as a corporation, her talent was so recognizable that she was promoted to the corporate headquarters and the store was left in the hands of a new store manager. Neither Minori nor I knew the new store manager very well. We both missed Lisa.[10]

---

10   To be clear, the First and Pike Starbucks has had a couple of different store managers. The first store manager of this store is currently at the SSC. The store manager who was present during the episode described here was only the store manager for a little under a year before moving on. And so again that store received a new store manager. I think it's stabilized now that I write this in 2014, but there was a time when

It was a strange connection. We knew the same person from different moments in time at the same store. Starbucks is a very small world.

Minori has a tradition of taking photos of himself standing next to Starbucks store managers and other Starbucks partners. Since his Seattle trips occurred no more than once a year, he memorialized them so he could remember each trip with tons of photos. If Minori had been transported back in time to the mid-1990s, all these moments at Starbucks would be his collection of Kodak Moments. He hoped for another great First and Pike Kodak Moment on this trip.

Partners all over Seattle have stood next to Minori for a picture. He kept all of those photos in a 3-ring binder that I was fortunate enough to see. It was like a trip down memory lane for me. I know many of the same Starbucks partners that he met over the years.

At the First and Pike Starbucks that day, the new store manager wouldn't come out from behind the bar for a photo with Minori. He scowled at us and mumbled something like, "You can take my picture at the espresso machine."

To this day, I don't know why he refused. It looked to me like he could've come out but customers don't always have a clear picture of what's happening inside a store at any given time. Maybe he really was too busy. My heart sank a bit for Minori. He left disappointed. Partner photos were a big deal to him. Minori said he still crossed his fingers for the chance to get his photo taken standing next Howard.

Even with this disappointment, we sat at the First and Pike Starbucks and talked like old friends. We turned our attention back to the half a dozen Starbucks paper bags. One was for me. I opened it up and thanked Minori for my Kyoto city coffee tumbler. As the two of us talked at the

First and Pike seemed to go through a store managers quicker than you can say Venti Caramel Macchiato.

names on the bags, I saw that he brought presents for a number of people who were above the store level and worked in the corporate headquarters. It seemed as if the partners that he had connected with the most were the ones who were most likely to get promoted to the corporate office.[11]

How in the world we were going to get presents to the Starbucks headquarters (also known as the Starbucks Support Center or SSC) on a Memorial Day holiday? The SSC is closed. I had to think about that one.[12]

With that question still hanging over our heads, Minori and I decided to head towards 15th Avenue Coffee and Tea for their morning cupping at 11:00 AM. I was driving since I knew my way around well (or I thought I did) and Minori was in the passenger seat. We were half way between 15th Avenue Coffee and Tea and the First and Pike Starbucks when suddenly it dawned on me that if I could reach someone who worked at the SSC, that would work. We didn't need to hand deliver each gift to its recipient. If we could drop the gifts off with anyone at the SSC that would work.

I had Andrew Fried's business card in my wallet. Andrew was the Regional Vice President for the Pacific Northwest. I had run into him in a book store in Pioneer Square two months before and fortuitously, I still had his card with me. I'd run into him in the past at 15th Avenue Coffee and Tea. In fact, that was where I had first met him. His business card included his cell phone number.

I fumbled with the phone number and drove up a steep hill at the same

---

11   True to Minori's knack of knowing who should be promoted, in 2013, one of the store managers Minori particularly liked was promoted from store manager to the Coffee Engagement Team at the SSC.

12   If this had happened in 2014, not 2010, I realize it would have been an easier task to get the presents to the SSC. By 2014, I knew more people at the headquarters than in 2010.

time. I know. Not safe or smart. This was before hands-free laws and before I owned a car with a Bluetooth feature. When Andrew Fried answered, I recognized his voice immediately. I explained our predicament: Minori had presents for a number of SSC partners and was at the end of a trip from Japan and he needed to get the presents delivered to the headquarters.

Andrew could not have been more gracious. "Leave them at 15th Avenue Coffee and Tea," he said. "I can swing by and pick them up on my way into the SSC tomorrow." It was a perfect solution to the present dilemma. Secretly, there was something about Andrew Fried that melted me a bit. He was smart, kind, and charismatic. But I think it was his southern drawl that got me.

Minori gestured and whispered that he wanted to talk to Andrew too. Regardless of whether you speak English or Japanese, there are some universal cell phone gestures. I thanked Andrew and handed the phone to Minori, who continued to talk with him as I drove. They were talking a bit about Starbucks' relationship with (Red). The (Red) organization fights AIDS in developing countries, and is funded by private donations, the sale of (Red) branded products, and large corporate sponsors, such as Starbucks. At one time, Starbucks offered a (Red) blend coffee, (Red) CD, and (Red) tumbler all with a percentage of the profits from those products donated to the (Red) organization.

It sounded like Minori was asking for the co-branded Starbucks-(Red) products to be introduced to Japan. "Bring a (Red) Starbucks card to Japan," Minori suggested in broken English. When customers paid with the co-branded (Red) Starbucks card, Starbucks donated five cents from each transaction to the (Red) organization.[13]

---

13   As of January 1, 2012 Starbucks stopped contributing $0.05 per transaction if you used the RED Starbucks Card. http://www.starbucks.

Pretty soon we were at 15th Avenue Coffee and Tea and the phone call with Andrew Fried ended. We dropped off the presents, leaving them in the care of the store's baristas. Trusty green aprons save the day! It was no problem. The partners there rolled with the flow and of course they knew Andrew well.

Minori and I joined in a coffee cupping. It was Minori's first cupping. He took a ton of photos. The world of Starbucks constantly involves photos. This store was a hub for meeting people in that 2009 – 2010 era, and so we were fortunate enough to experience a coffee cupping led by a twenty-year Starbucks partner. After dropping off presents and participating in the cupping, we were on our way to the next Starbucks on our list.

I picked our next Starbucks-tourist-destination: The Fourth Avenue South and Diagonal Avenue South Starbucks in the SODO neighborhood. I've always felt like that was a bit of an under-appreciated store.

The Fourth and Diagonal location opened in the summer of 2008. Starbucks used that store as an early prototype store to experiment with alternate design ideas. Because of this, it doesn't look quite like any other Starbucks. It was one of the first stores to get a huge community table made from reclaimed wood. The community table has a large natural split in the wood, giving it tremendous character. The store has hanging signs with words in a few different languages and abstract leaf patterns. It has large local area photographs showing off how industrial the SODO neighborhood is. The drive-thru is incredibly long with photos of partners and coffee-themed images. It looks a bit like a Disneyland ride due to the tremendous amount of signage. This drive-thru is the "It's a Small World" ride of the land of Starbucks Drive-Thrus.

com/responsibility/community/starbucks-red

Unfortunately, I didn't realize the store would be closed on Memorial Day. All the adjacent businesses were closed too. We got out of the car and peeked in the windows. At one point, we both had our noses right up against the glass windows of the store, peering inside as best we could, and making some ooh and aaahhh noises as we looked at hanging banners and the beautiful community table. I'm sure the next day, some young barista in a green apron wondered how the windows got so smudged. We walked away, leaving nose prints, complete handprints, and fingerprints as evidence of our excursion. Minori tried to get some photos of that amazing reclaimed-wood table in the store but it was too dark inside for pictures.

From the 4th and Diagonal Starbucks we drove to the Mariner's souvenir store so that Minori could stock up on Mariner's baseball logoed stuff to take back to Japan. I think these were more gifts for his friends and family back in Japan. Generosity was fundamental to Minori's way of being.

Although we only spent a few hours together, it was completely enjoyable. My office is in Pioneer Square, not far from the stadiums so we dropped by there too. Slowly, my small office has turned into its own kind of Starbucks museum, with the walls adorned with Starbucks posters, and a million cups and mugs. Minori had the chance to visit the Via Bearista Bear, which sat upright with its feet in an 18-ounce Starbucks coffee mug.

Finally he had to go. When people don't understand how I stay motivated to blog, I always refer back on experiences like this. I made a friend in Minori. The passion he showed for Starbucks during this short visit humbled me.

I did follow up with Andrew Fried, and sure enough the regional director was more reliable than Santa Claus: All the presents from Japan got delivered to the all the right people at the Starbucks headquarters.

Give of your time and give to others (regardless of whether it's Memorial Day!)

Chapter Ten: The Coffee Spill (AKA On Meeting Cliff)

Eons ago, before I started my blog, a former Starbucks store partner told me a story about meeting Cliff Burrows at the Fourth and Seneca Starbucks. In the past, Cliff Burrows was *President of Starbucks North America*. It seemed like a year went by, and then he had had an even bigger title: *Starbucks President of the Americas*. And then his title swelled again. Officially, his bio currently states the following. "*As group president, U.S., Americas, and Teavana, Cliff Burrows is responsible for all of Starbucks operations in the United States, Canada, and Latin America, as well as the expansion of Teavana retail stores and the integration of Teavana into Starbucks retail stores.*" I've stopped trying to memorize his title. In this book I'll refer to Cliff as *President of Just About Everything Starbucks* from now and then. It's how I think of him and I think that adequately sums up his job description. Should he go through yet another promotion, I'll still frequently refer to him as President of *Just About Everything Starbucks*. The tall, graying man with a Welsh accent and spectacles is in charge of a boatload of Starbucks.

But let's get back to the story. I tell this with the cautionary warning that I wasn't there when this episode happened.

A meeting was scheduled at the Fourth and Seneca Starbucks and Cliff arrived early. With his eyes focused on store cleanliness, he couldn't help but notice that cigarette butts littered the sidewalk at the front entrance to the store along busy Fourth Avenue. Every store partner was too busy to run outside and sweep the cigarette butts. Cliff, seeing this, grabbed the broom and dustbin and went outside to do the job himself.

When I heard this story, I thought for sure there was some exaggeration going on. I'm naturally suspicious of hearsay – that is, when you tell a story not based upon what you personally experienced, but based upon what you heard someone say. This was the only story I'd heard about him before I met him. I loathe to listen to hearsay, yet this story impressed me and I hoped it was true.

In May 2010, I met Cliff at 15th Avenue Coffee and Tea. I recognized him from the annual meetings of shareholders, seeing him in the news now and then, and from his executive profile on the official Starbucks. com webpage about the senior leadership team.

We made nothing more than small talk. I told him how much I had liked the product Sorbetto and that I was disappointed that it never launched nationally. Sorbetto was a tangy frozen treat that was a bit like a very soft ice cream or frozen yogurt. Italian-inspired, it came in small ten ounce servings, and was offered in two flavors: Tangy Sorbetto or Citrus Ice Sorbetto. I had tried Sorbetto when it was in its test phase. It had been tested in a few stores north of Seattle, and I stumbled upon it there. In addition, Sorbetto went through a large-scale regional test in a number of Southern California locations sometime in 2008 - 2009. Lucky for me, on trips home to Orange County to visit family, I discovered it was widely available in Starbucks stores. My sister-in-law and brother got tired of me pestering them every five minutes to go to Starbucks.

"Can we go to Starbucks now? There's something in your stores not available in Seattle…"

I understood why Sorbetto had failed to make it to a national product launch. By 2010, Sorbetto was dead in the water as future Starbucks product. I heard gossip from partners as to the reasons why it didn't do well-everything from customers didn't want an expensive small dessert at Starbucks during a recession to the equipment used to dispense Sorbetto took up too much counter space and was extraordinarily labor intensive to clean.

Despite all this, I liked the way it tasted. Bring on the Sorbetto. I was ready for it. "Yes, it was a good product," Cliff agreed, as we sat at the store's community table and he patiently listened to me explain how I dreamed of Sorbetto making its way into Seattle Starbucks. It was delicious. He explained to me a few points why Sorbetto wouldn't work in stores, though it was a story I already knew.

I learned a lesson from Sorbetto. Until that point, I hadn't realized that Starbucks often has small tests running all over the country, and that few items make it out of a test phase to a national product launch. Just like the Honey Vanilla Vivanno in 2009 (which never made it out of a tiny California testing phase), there are constant tests in Starbucks, even today. As I learned more and more about Starbucks, I slowly began to appreciate that beverages and products needed to have several key characteristics. They had to have wide-spread appeal nationally. They had to be offered at a price point that would be attractive to customers and produce acceptable profit margins to Starbucks. And they couldn't create bottlenecks in sourcing ingredients across 12,000 United States stores. This balance was a trick in and of itself. Finding that perfect next hit beverage or food item, meeting all of the above requirements, was in part the result of meticulous planning, testing, and probably involved at least a little bit of luck.

On this spring day at 15th Avenue Coffee and Tea, Cliff and I had dropped by for the same reason: to congratulate a Starbucks partner on fifteen years with Starbucks. After the Sorbetto-infused small talk, we made our way toward the fifteen-year partner, where chocolate cake, coffee, and effusive congratulations all were in order.

Mr. Long Term Partner regaled us with tales of when the Frappuccino was still new in stores and baristas brewed Starbucks Italian Roast Coffee double strength to make the Frappuccino liquid base. "There was no whipped cream in stores back then…" he went on to tell us. The conversation flowed. Many people told their stories of Starbucks of yesteryear, including scooping beans from bins, individually bagging each pound of coffee, affixing the correct coffee sticker on the plain white bag, and writing the date on the packaging while reminding customers that beans should be used within seven days of purchase. All of this for great coffee at-home enjoyment.

Nostalgia is a funny thing. We fondly and selectively remember the best of the past. But a business that too fiercely clings to nostalgia runs the risk of becoming stagnant and dull. Something new has to be around the corner. Just as the Disneyland that I remember repeatedly visiting in the 1970s has gone through major changes, Starbucks too must keep up with the time. Sure I have some nostalgia for Disneyland "E-Tickets[14]," and rides and attractions long gone, such as America Sings and the Adventure Through Innerspace ride, what's replaced it is better and more current for today.

The stories of Starbucks yesteryear continued. Someone offered, "Can you imagine? We thought if a customer wanted to go a little crazy with their Frappuccino, we'd add a shot of espresso and call it an Espresso Frappuccino."

---

14   In the 1970s, when you visited Disneyland in Anaheim, a visitor paid an admission fee and separate fee to buy tickets for each ride. Visitors bought books of tickets with a small number of variety of tickets. The most exciting and popular rides were "E-Ticket" rides.

At the right intervals there was chuckling and laughter. The filled-to-the-brim hot coffee in my right hand wasn't up for hearty giggles. I spilled a not-insignificant amount of liquid onto the floor in the midst of this Starbucks history lesson.

It happened so fast. Cliff, The President of Just About Everything Starbucks, unceremoniously reached down and wiped the spill with the napkin in his hand. It took no longer than five seconds, and for all of two seconds I was staring at the top of Cliff's head. In the time it took for me to track both the hand-scooped coffee bean conversation and deduce where the nearest paper towels might be, the coffee spill was gone.

I flashbacked to the story I'd heard about Cliff sweeping up cigarette butts in front of the Fourth and Seneca Street Starbucks. In that split second, the thought occurred to me: Cliff would never ask a partner to do something he wouldn't do himself. He'll clean and sweep like anyone else, if the moment in time calls for it.

The conversation quieted a bit as a number of people enjoyed the cake that had been brought for the occasion, and all went back to normal. The significance of the moment lingered with me.

A leader knows how to hold both the broom to sweep the floor and the pen to enact innovation, and willingly will use either one, as needed.

Chapter Eleven: December 2010 Visit With Minori

Lucky for me, Minori took another trip to Seattle in December of 2010. It was shortly before Christmas and I took a day off from work in the middle of the week so that I would have all day to visit with him. I didn't want to have a rushed few hours on a holiday when numerous businesses were closed.

We met up that morning at 15th Avenue Coffee and Tea again: an easy meeting spot. As Minori had come all the way from Japan for this Starbucks adventure, I told him that I would follow along with whatever plans for the day that he had. I explained that I had taken the day off work, and we could do as he liked. We grabbed food and coffee and came up with a game plan for the day. Minori had some definite ideas in mind.

"We have to find the Verona Bridge in Seattle," Minori said.

I didn't know there was a Verona Bridge in Seattle. I knew there was a bridge featured on the Caffè Verona[15] whole bean packaging, but I didn't know if it was real, or where the bridge was. How did Minori know this obscure bit of Starbucks trivia? I was amazed at Minori's wealth of knowledge about Starbucks.

Minori went on to explain that the picture of the bridge on the coffee packaging for Caffè Verona was a real bridge in Seattle, and told me as

---

15   The Caffè Verona packaging now features a rose as its main icon. I miss the Verona Bridge imagery.

much as he knew about it.

Neither Minori nor I knew *exactly* where the mysterious Verona Bridge was. This was the problem. Together we deduced that it had to be in Seattle's Arboretum Park, but that still was a lot of ground to cover. Two hundred and thirty acres to be exact. Even worse, Minori didn't know where Seattle's Arboretum was, and I was embarrassed to admit that it had been many years since I'd visited the Arboretum. Would I end up lost in my own city?

We piled into the car and headed east from 15th Avenue Coffee and Tea because I was sure that was at least the right general direction. But suddenly I was stumped. It's a big park. You can't miss it. Yet somehow I had no idea where to go.

We had no in-car navigation to guide us. I did something I've done often over the years. I picked up my cell phone and called Jack, The Tower Crane Operator, also known as my significant other. He was born and raised in Seattle. Been here his whole life.

Over the years, I discovered I had no need for in-car navigation or AAA roadside services. Jack had rescued me from the side of the road more than once. Directions in Seattle were always one phone call away. Jack knew every road. Jack is from the Baby Boomer generation and sometimes he'd say things to me like, "I remember as a kid watching the Seattle Center being built and watching the cement trucks roll in." It's only fitting that he ended up being a builder of tall buildings, bridges, and things made of rebar and concrete.

Right now I needed the Map-Guide-Version of Jack. He was within easy reach. He was two-hundred and fifty feet high in the sky, sitting in a tower crane, building an annex to Swedish Hospital.

He guided us right to the park, and planted us within a few hundred feet of the bridge. Even though my car has built-in navigation now, I still call Jack.

Looking for the bridge no longer seemed mysterious. Once we found our way to Lake Washington Boulevard, the bridge was obvious. I had probably driven right under it before and never noticed the famous bridge from the Verona whole bean coffee packaging.

It's a beautiful old bridge with a canopy of trees on both sides. This bridge really does look like it could be in Italy. The official City of Seattle Parks Department name is the Wilcox Footbridge. Nonetheless, it will always be the Verona Bridge to me.

Much later, I confirmed with a former Starbucks design partner that they'd staged some photos with Starbucks partners standing on the bridge and used it for an artistic rendering on the coffee packaging.

We took pictures, climbed the stairs to the bridge, and walked back and forth over it. We tweeted a few photos of the beautiful bridge. Minori asked me to stand on the bridge on the same place where the figures on the coffee packaging stood. The Verona Bridge fun was as wonderful as kids playing at recess. I hope the memories of this day never leave me.

After the Verona Bridge adventure, we got back on Lake Washington Boulevard which eventually connects with Madison Street. Our next stop was the Madison Park Starbucks.

Midday, and in the middle of the week, the Starbucks was slow. I ordered a Vivanno Smoothie and Minori ordered tea. We sat, chatting for a bit. "This is Howard Schultz's Starbucks – apparently he visits this store all the time," I told Minori.

We were officially stalking Howard Schultz's store. I knew how much Minori still wanted to meet Howard. I secretly hoped that he would walk in the door and yell, "Surprise!" and Minori would have the chance to shake his hand and tell Howard how much he loved Starbucks.

But unfortunately Howard Schultz did not appear. When you want to run into him, you can't.

We weren't done yet though. There was still another stop on this day-long Starbucks adventure. Minori picked the Starbucks located at 1301 Second Avenue, in downtown Seattle, for a visit. It's located on the second floor of the Russell Investment Center at Second and Union. We were heading back into an area of Seattle that I knew very well.

"What's so special about the Second and Union Starbucks?" I asked him. I was confused.

"Pumpkin Spice Latte," he said.

I had no idea what he was talking about. I doubted my prowess as a Starbucks fan.

"A Pumpkin Spice Latte commercial!"

I was still lost. At this point, I was earning failing marks as a Starbucks aficionado. And even more curious, Minori was suddenly grabbing green straws at the condiment bar and trying to play air drums with them.

I did the only logical thing I could think of. I pulled out my iPad and did a Google search on "Pumpkin Spice Latte commercial." There it was: this weird, less-than-one-minute long commercial with a guy talking about the Pumpkin Spice Latte and drumming with Starbucks straws in the air.

Meet Charles. He's a big fan of the Pumpkin Spice Latte at Starbucks and he really wants to talk to you about it.[16]

I wasn't sure I could stomach the full fifty seconds of Charles, but if Minori wanted to see the store where this commercial was filmed, that would be our next stop. The commercial seemed cheesy and unbelievable to me. Perhaps I needed remedial Pumpkin Spice Latte fandom lessons. I wasn't even a huge fan of that seasonal beverage, though I was aware it was one of Starbucks' best sellers year after year. Many people

---

16   http://youtu.be/-KbYiHm8A3Y

mark the introduction of fall weather with their first Pumpkin Spice Latte of the year. The hype and phenomena was lost on me, and so the commercial held no allure.

I never did figure out how Minori knew which Starbucks in Seattle that Pumpkin Spice latte commercial was filmed at.

When we arrived at the Second and Union Starbucks, there were three partners working. I ordered a Caramel Brûlée Latte and Minori ordered hot tea again. Minori explained he needed a soothing drink and that he was already feeling worn out from the day's adventures.

It seemed sacrilegious not to order a Pumpkin Spice Latte but it was late December, and no longer the season of Pumpkin Spice[17]. We took a bunch of photos of the interior of the store, even some with Minori posing like the character Charles in the Pumpkin Spice Latte commercial playing air drums with the longer Venti cold beverage length green straws.

One of the Second and Union store baristas remembered that commercial filming there. She said that the film crew came in after the store was closed, moved the condiment stations around, and filmed until early in the morning. Our useless knowledge about Pumpkin Spice Latte commercials grew.

We were coming to the end of a great day. Minori was tired. We walked to the next closest Starbucks, located inside Seattle's Benaroya Hall,

---

17   Starbucks tends to have repeat, well-loved seasonal drinks. The fall season is the Pumpkin Spice Latte which can be ordered iced, hot or as a Frappuccino. The Christmas season holiday drinks usually include the Peppermint Mocha, Gingerbread Latte, Eggnog Latte, and Caramel Brûlée Latte. The holiday drink lineup can vary slightly depending on regional tests and regional demand, but for many customers, winter is marked by a festive red Starbucks cup and a Peppermint Mocha.

where the Seattle Symphony performs. I had parked in the Benaroya parking garage and it was time to head back to the car.

We sat inside the lobby of Benaroya Hall and I played with my iPad. I was beveraged out. Minori and I collapsed at a table and he drank one more hot tea. The lobby has a few kiosk storefronts, lots of tables and chairs, and Dale Chihuly's fine hand blown glass hanging from the ceiling.

"Minori, this is a great vacation! I hope someday I get to come to Japan and visit Starbucks stores there with you."

Minori turned melancholy. It was a surprising change of demeanor. His face lost all its joy in the space of a breath.

"This is not a vacation."

"What do you mean?" I was puzzled. It looked and felt like a vacation from my perspective.

"No. I'm sick. I can't work. I have cancer."

I was stunned. I'm sure the color drained from my face too. He went on to explain to me that he was healing from a surgery. I felt worry, sadness, and fatigue all at the same time.

"I fight the cancer," Minori said to me, confidently.

I tried to probe into the specifics of what kind of cancer. Starbucks is like a universal language that many speak. Probably the world over, many people can say "Double Tall Latte." Although Minori's English was very good, the words for body parts and medical procedures didn't come to him.

Minori pulled the iPad out of my hand and pretty soon was doing Google searches. The next thing I knew, he was pointing at images of the human colon that turned up in his search results.

We left the lobby in a somber mood. All I could do was worry. And I made Minori promise that if ever needed anything from me, he would ask.

Cherish every moment.

Chapter Twelve: We Have Won in so Many Ways

It was January 2011. Starbucks made world-wide news when they announced they would change their logo. The new logo would free the famous twin-tailed Starbucks Siren from her cage of the words "Starbucks Coffee."

The media was all over this story. Some thought it was the end of Starbucks Coffee as we know it. Stories of 15th Avenue Coffee and Tea had already been in the news. There were Starbucks stores that sold beer and wine. And so the logo change – specifically dropping the words Starbucks Coffee from around the green Siren – to some meant that Starbucks was no longer going to be about coffee. As if you might walk into a grocery store and find a Starbucks Light Beer wedged between a Budweiser and Miller Genuine Draft. Commentators and customers worried that Starbucks would no longer be judicious about which widgets, beverages and food items you'd find the Starbucks logo slapped on.

I had moments of worry too and I'm sure I vocalized that a time or two. Would there be Starbucks smoothie mixes, coffee creamers or cereal? But I trusted that Starbucks would get it right.

The official unveiling of the logo took place at the Seattle headquarters at 2401 Utah Avenue South. I was lucky to attend. I listened to Howard Schultz speak and recorded a tiny section of his presentation with my smart phone.

"We have won in many ways," Howard said. "But I feel it is so important to constantly remind us all of how fleeting success and winning can be if we don't continue to operate with the same level of hunger, of passion, of belief, in pursuit of excellence and not settle for mediocrity. There are literally 200,000 people who in many ways rely collectively on what we do here every day. And inversely, we rely on the 200,000 people and everything that goes on outside of this building – on them – to execute a strategy more often than not that we create. You have built – you have built – an extraordinary company that literally is recognized and respected all over the world. But as I have said so many times: it is not an entitlement. We have to earn it. And we learned the hard way two and half years ago that we have to earn it every day. So I ask you, more than anything else, to remember the feeling of what it was like when the world had pretty much turned against us and people stopped believing in who we were and who we could be. Because it was the resilience and the belief in one another, our core purpose, our mission, our values, the quality of our coffee and the experience, and everything we have created over forty years that we have transformed to be in this place. I now believe, and this is not something I am just saying, that our best days as a company and as an organization are absolutely in front of us. The opportunities that are going to avail themselves to the company, and to the individuals who are going to create all this, it's going to be quite significant. But those opportunities have to be earned. And I ask you individually and collectively, as I did in New Orleans, to understand what it means to take the work personally and to be responsible. And when you see something that you know is inconsistent with the quality and the excellence of the heritage of this company, don't be a bystander. You have a voice. It doesn't matter who you are in the company and how long you have worked here: you are a Starbucks partner. You have a voice. And we need everyone's com-

mitment, and everyone's voice to continue to succeed at the level we have achieved over the last few years. And I promise that what I am asking of you, I am asking of myself in the exact same way. That we will continue to work together to build the kind of company that you and your family will be extremely proud of in the future years to come. But I guarantee you, the future of Starbucks has significant promise and we are just getting started. Thank you very much."

You have a voice. Don't be a bystander. Work together. They were great words, regardless of your chosen career. I was inspired.

It takes every single person on the team to succeed.

Chapter Thirteen: How to Get a T-Shirt

It was March in Seattle and I was grateful it wasn't raining. I'd been standing in line outside McCaw Hall for an hour with my friend Rose. I wondered again why we felt compelled to arrive so early every year. The doors opened at 8:00 AM, but the 2011 Starbucks Shareholder's Meeting wouldn't start until 10:00 AM. Still, the free coffee and people-watching was good.

I own a few shares of Starbucks stock, mainly for the opportunity to attend the annual meeting. Rose is a long-timer, having bought stock in 1992 at the initial public offering. With us in line were a varied group of shareholders, most of whom own many more shares than I can dream of. There were corporate types in fine suits, older men and women who look like they could be dressed for a night at the Seattle Symphony, and a few young Starbucks partners who want the opportunity to soak up an annual Starbucks meeting. What unites us is a passion for Starbucks and a vested interest in its success.

Together we waited patiently outside McCaw Hall. Well, Rose waited patiently, anyway. Sipping her coffee contentedly, she admired the modern glass-paned building that serves as home to the Seattle Opera, the Pacific Northwest Ballet, and the Starbucks' annual shareholder meeting. I, on the other hand, was ready to burst with anticipation. Starbucks is known for its entertaining annual meetings. I'd never been to any other company's shareholder meetings, but I figured that most were dreadfully dull. Imagine going to a Black & Decker annual meeting. I rest my case. Rose contradicted me, though. She recounted her experience at a Whole Foods annual meeting where she ended up with a huge sack of freebie groceries. It sounded good, but still I think Starbucks meetings are probably more fun.

Starbucks annual meetings have it all: famous celebrity singers, great coffee and food, dense presentations with lots of numbers, enticing sneak peeks at new offerings, enthusiastic pronouncements about Starbucks' future, and best of all, the concluding question-and-answer period. Over the years, celebrities like K.D. Lang and Sheryl Crow have come out to perform at Starbucks annual meetings. It's a concert and an annual meeting all rolled into one. But the only truly ad-hoc, spontaneous part of the meeting is the Q & A session, because you never know what someone will ask Howard Schultz, Cliff Burrows, and the rest of the senior leadership team. In past years, I've heard the gamut. Why doesn't Via Ready Brew come in a jar? Will you have pizza in stores? Would you please make a sugar-free whipped cream? And you never know what the reply will be. It's a surprisingly comedic ending to the day.

While I waited. I debated whether I should get up and throw out a question during the Q & A session. I didn't have a burning question. If I didn't ask a question at the meeting, I might still be able to get one answered through Mallory, one of my contacts in the Starbucks Public Relations department. But there was a big difference between a PR email reply and a first-hand answer from the senior leadership team. I wanted the chance to ask Howard a question. Maybe I could erase my memory of that terrible first meeting. Or his.

"Rose, what if I ask which Via Ready Brew is most popular? Does it do well in every country?"

"You could, Melody. Drinking water might be more interesting."

Okay, I guess I won't ask that question.

When we entered McCaw Hall, I noticed that almost every partner was wearing a white t-shirt which featured the word "ONWARD" in green lettering. I was immediately jealous even though I thought they must be chilly in March in Seattle. Rose and I meandered the halls, drank, ate, and enjoyed socializing until the meeting began. Then two hours of the meeting flew by. I learned about Starbucks' plan to partner with Keurig to create Starbucks K-cups, we heard about the success of MyStarbucksIdea.com, and we *oohed* and *aahed* over pictures of foods and beverages offered in international stores. It turned out that in one Asian market, you could get a Frappuccino that was half coffee and half tea.

Finally, the Q & A period arrived. One shareholder wanted to know about the success of beer and wine Starbucks stores, like 15th Avenue Coffee and Tea and a few other locations, such as the East Olive Way Starbucks. The 15th Avenue Coffee and Tea store had converted back into a logoed-Starbucks but kept beer and wine[18].

Facing my fear of public speaking, I bravely snuck into the line to ask the leadership team a question. In Washington State, A misdemeanor jury has six people on it[19]. For me personally, I've often thought that six was the highest number of people that I could comfortably address. Above six people, my palms sweat a little.

After several others, it was my turn. There I was in a suit, trying to look as polished as can be, asking a question of Howard Schultz.

"Howard, in years past, Starbucks has partnered with many great

---

18   By 2014, the Starbucks once known as 15th Avenue Coffee and Tea removed beer and wine from their lineup. However, Starbucks expanded beer and wine offerings at a number of other stores where it did sell well.

19   The size of a misdemeanor jury can vary from state to state.

good-cause organizations." I paused, looking at my list of organizations. "There's been (RED), and CARE, and Conservation International. Howard, do you have a favorite partnership or one that you're really sentimental about?"

I genuinely thought it would be fun to know which good-cause partnership has been most meaningful to Howard, but he dodged my question. It was clear he didn't want to be pinned down to one answer. I might as well have asked him to pick a favorite child, or a favorite store. After Howard answered, I seized the opportunity to ask one more thing, despite the strict rule of one question per person. Quickly, without thinking, I blurted out, "Hey, how can I get one of those Onward t-shirts?"

He chuckled. "Melody, we'll get you a t-shirt." And my turn was over.

A young woman in a sharp suit approached the microphone to address Howard Schultz and the leadership team next. She had some serious heels on. She meant business.

"I am a self-starter," she began. She told the audience that she was passionate about Starbucks. "I have a great education, and recently got my MBA." She outlined her resume. Ah, this is what makes the Q&A session so interesting. People can say whatever they want. There's no script. It's like improv comedy meets Wall Street business. I continued to listen to her and it dawned on me: she wanted a job.

"Can I get a job at Starbucks headquarters?

Howard didn't miss a beat. Deadpan, he replied, "Are you sure you wouldn't rather just have a t-shirt?"

The room broke into laughter. Who knew that Howard was a master of one-liners?

A week later, a box showed up at my workplace. In it was the ONWARD t-shirt and a note from Mallory wishing me well. I think it's amazing that I didn't have to do any follow up at all. I didn't even confirm an address[20], yet sure enough the t-shirt showed up, exactly as promised.

I have no idea if the woman in the business suit got a job. But I got an ONWARD t-shirt.

If you don't ask, you don't know what the answer will be.

---

20   Over a few years' time, I got to know Mallory who was amazingly generous with her time and energy. It was because of her reaching out to me that I was able to do fun things like attend the unveiling of the new logo in January 2011. She appreciated my blog and kept her eyes open for fun things for me to do with Starbucks. If I had a question about something, she'd answer the phone at 5:15 and respond to emails any time of the day. While I didn't expect all the extra work she did, it definitely didn't go unnoticed.

Chapter Fourteen: Pens, Pens, Pens (March 8, 2011, Part I)

The Starbucks Coffee Gear Store is inside the corporate headquarters. Anyone can go shopping for logoed t-shirts, pens, unique tasting cups, key chains, magnets, sweatshirts, and much more. Once in a while, you'll find a Starbucks umbrella or cycling jersey there too. For many years, the Coffee Gear Store was buried deep inside the inner sanctum of the corporate headquarters and the only way to get to it was to be escorted by a corporate partner who stood around while the guest shopped. Non-employees rarely ever went shopping there. The logistics of this arrangement – having to know a corporate partner and be escorted by him or her – didn't make a lot of sense for a store that wanted to sell more and be open to the general public.

I've shopped there a couple of times, but not often as I would like. The store's hours are Monday through Friday, so whether they're open to the public or not, I can't easily leave work and to run to the Coffee Gear Store, despite that 2401 Utah Avenue South is only short distance from my office.

In 2011, the Coffee Gear Store underwent a major remodel. On March 8th, it reopened in a new location at the Starbucks headquarters. Now it's near the main front reception desk so that customers can easily walk in and shop without the hassle of a Starbucks partner escort.

I attended the grand re-opening on March 8, 2011. Mallory, a PR person who often reached out to me, invited me to check out the remodel and offered to show me around. I could have gone on my own later on, but it was much more fun to be with Mallory, whom I knew and liked. There were several events happening at Starbucks in March, all related to their "Fortieth Anniversary Celebration." It was a busy day for Starbucks.

I spent quite a while at the Coffee Gear Store. I couldn't decide between buying Starbucks logo sweatshirts and t-shirts, magnets, journals, or a variety of pens and highlighters. There were too many choices. Thankfully, Mallory was incredibly patient as she too appeared to be checking out its new location, and offerings.

I liked all the pens – the ones word-marked with Starbucks, the ones with the Siren, and the ones with a combination of both the word-mark and the logo. I wanted to buy volumes of these pens. I write a lot for my job, and I knew that I'd be the only person at the courthouse with Starbucks-branded pens in my briefcase.

Standing in front of a wall of pens, my senses were on overload and didn't know if I should grab them by the handful or be more cautious in my spending.

In the middle of my dilemma, in walked Howard Schultz. He was with Cameron, the executive vice president of global communications. I recognized him as well, having met him at previous shareholder meetings. I was shopping for pens. Maybe they needed some pens too. At that moment, I firmly decided my best option was to *completely* ignore them. Pretend Howard wasn't there. Mallory too didn't interject in Howard's visit to the Coffee Gear Store. She continued to shop in another corner of the store. Howard had a familiar *I'm busy* look plastered on his face that said, "I don't have time for autographs and small talk right now." Perhaps a friendly "Hello Howard" was in order, but I knew today was a big day. Mallory had primed me that Howard would soon be giving an afternoon speech in celebration of Starbucks' Fortieth Anniversary and he would also be the special guest of honor ringing the official NASDAQ bell for the close of the Wall Street markets[21]. The look on his face made sense to me. I didn't think today would be a good day for yet another episode of tugging on Superman's cape.

Concentrate on the pens, Melody, I thought. I picked a few up, then put them back down, as if writing in blue ink or black ink might be a terribly big decision for me.

Howard and Cameron were talking amongst themselves, but they were quiet enough that I really couldn't hear what was being said. *Pens, pens, pens*, I thought.

Howard spent a few minutes looking around, seemingly giving the newly-remodeled store his nod of approval. Out of the corner of my eye, I saw them turn to go, Cameron two steps ahead of Howard.

Suddenly, Howard stopped cold at the entrance of the store and turned, facing me. "Hey Melody," he shouted. I turned to face him, but frozen, in a moment of *What the hell?* He was *loud*. There is no doubt, when Howard Schultz yells at you, even if it ends up that he's kidding around, it's a frightening moment. I'm glad I didn't pee my pants.

"Hey Melody," Howard yelled, "Don't buy everything in the store! Leave something for the partners!" He had a huge, winning, smile on his

---

21   The NASDAQ is based in New York City, but the ceremonies can be done remotely with modern technology allowing remote ringing of the bell and special decorative podium designed for the event. In this way, NASDAQ has the ability to travel to allow CEOs of publicly traded corporations a moment for presentations and a remote ringing of the bell. The Starbucks bell ringing on March 8, 2011 is mentioned here: http://www.nasdaq.com/marketsite/03082011_close.html

face. He was totally playing with me.

And then he left out the door in a hustle and was gone.

Sometimes Superman tugs back.

Chapter Fifteen: Brand Days Tour (March 8, 2011 Part II)

Mallory and I left the Coffee Gear Store shopping excursion with a full grocery sack-sized bag of unique Starbucks merchandise.

Mallory didn't want me to miss a thing[22]. She hinted that she had more planned for my day at the headquarters. "Howard's speech and ringing of the NASDAQ Bell starts in about a half hour. You can store your bag of goodies at my desk so you don't have to carry it around with you. We'll be busy for a couple of hours." I followed her to a cubicle, where we planted my sack of pens, t-shirts, magnets and more on her office chair. Her thoughtfulness didn't go unnoticed. I was glad not to have to haul my Starbucks Coffee Gear store purchases around with me.

Together we headed to the front entrance of 2401 Utah Avenue South. In the same spot where I'd once attended a Via Ready Brew kick off in 2009, Mallory and I listened to speeches by Howard and others, and watched the ringing of the NASDAQ bell. Howard personally thanked every Starbucks partner with more than twenty years of service to the company. Each twenty-year partner was singled out and asked to stand near Howard by the stage. The crowd also heard of Howard's plan to

---

22   Mallory is amazing. About every eight weeks or so, a half-pound of the most recent Reserve Coffee offering would show up at my office with a note from her, reminding me that she shared a passion for Starbucks coffee.

turn every April into a Global Month of Service, with large-scale volunteering events and an emphasis on giving back to local communities where Starbucks operates. A Starbucks executive in charge of coordinating community service introduced special guests in the audience. There were a few customer invitees who were directors of local non-profits and charities.

To top it off, March 8, 2011 also marked the introduction of a new coffee in honor of forty years: Tribute Blend Coffee[23].

The hour flew by, the closing bell had been rung, and hundreds of partners made their way back into the headquarters to return to work. It had been a full day with Howard Schultz ringing both the opening and closing NASDAQ bell[24], and a lot of other activities in between.

Mallory found me in the thinning crowd and said, "There's more." I followed her and headed in the direction of the Starbucks parking garage. We were joined by about six or seven other customers who seemed to also be escorted by Starbucks partners. As I looked around, I saw that a few of the faces were the community leaders who had been introduced, but I don't recall their names nor did I recognize their partner escorts.

Sure enough, the five minute walk took us to a floor of the Starbucks parking garage. Our small group stopped at the entrance of a temporary exhibit. A Starbucks marketing executive, whom I recognized but didn't

---

23   http://www.starbucks.com/blog/666/a-tribute-to-40-years-of-coffee-with-you

24   http://www.globenewswire.com/news-release/2011/03/08/441781/215654/en/Starbucks-Corporation-SBUX-to-Conduct-NASDAQ-Opening-Bell-Ceremony-Remotely-From-Pike-Place-Market-Starbucks-Store-in-Seattle-Washington.html

really know, led us through the Starbucks Brand Day tour. We heard a strict rule that no photography was permitted during the exhibit. The marketing executive explained that the Brand Days Tour was designed to invigorate and inspire Starbucks partners, and that partners everywhere were invited any time to do a self-tour of the exhibit.

Starbucks had created a temporary museum on most of one floor of their parking garage. Partitions were set up to create rooms, and the exhibit allowed a person to tour the story of Starbucks as a brand.

I, along with the small select group of customers, walked through makeshift rooms with photos, cutting edge store designs, products exclusive to international stores, displays showing how social media is important to Starbucks, and rooms of CPG items (consumer packaged goods-the types of Starbucks products you might find in grocery stores). There was room with digital displays showing things that customers said about Starbucks using hashtags and a room set up with current store furniture design. The social media monitors impressed me. I love the examples of customer connections.

The most fascinating room had a large dining room-sized wood table set up with perhaps thirty loose pieces of paper. Each one had an image of the Starbucks siren. These were the designs of the new logo that were rejected before the 2011 logo was revealed. It was weird to see the Starbucks siren in profile, or to see her in new colors, or her hair flowing all over the place. The Starbucks creative department had explored all options before the final 2011 version of the Starbucks[25] logo was approved.

I badly wanted to take a picture of the Siren logo rejects. I nagged at

---

25   The 2011 version of the Starbucks logo is the version that now most people think of when they think of Starbucks. It's simply the Siren free of the words and the ring that used to say "Starbucks Coffee" surrounding her.

Mallory. "One photo with my phone?" The answer was no.

The last room of the Brand Days tour contained a wall of hanging cups. They were strung together, hung from the ceiling, and spanned about a twelve-foot long wall. The cups were the classic Starbucks hot cups: white cups with the word Starbucks and the Starbucks siren on them.

Each cup was to be signed by a partner affirming his promise to the spirit of the brand. The partner could sign the wall behind the cups too. There was a small table of Sharpie pens nearby and there were still plenty of white cups. I was offered a pen to sign a cup and I turned it down. There was only so much wall space, and only so many cups would be displayed. I appreciated that the whole intent of the Brand Days Tour was to inspire partners, not customers. I watched as a few people around me signed the wall and cups.

The tour ended. My March 8, 2011, had been a day to remember. Mallory and I walked back to her desk.

"Thank you so much for coming today. I wanted you to experience our fortieth anniversary celebrations first hand," she said softly.

I should be the one thanking her, I thought. She handed me one more thing. One more gift. Inside a standard small Starbucks bag was a pound of Tribute Blend.

"You can't leave without coffee, can you?" My eyes got a little wet in the corners. In my mind, I was hearing her say the famous words, "We're in the people business serving coffee." It had been a good day.

More than three years went by before I saw those signed Starbucks cups again.

In December 2013, I was inside the SSC to visit someone from the PR department. Mallory wasn't available and so I arranged to meet with a new Starbucks PR representative to discuss coffee innovation. Despite that I have now been inside the Starbucks headquarters a number of times, I always have to follow closely behind the PR contact, otherwise I'd get lost. There should be a Starbucks headquarters map guide.

We strolled through the SSC late on a Friday, through an area of the building I hadn't seen before. In the middle of a large atrium, along a wall, I saw the display of signed cups from the Brand Days Tour. I recognized them immediately.

There were no unsigned cups anymore. I commented to my PR host, "Do you know the story behind these cups?" and she said that she didn't and that they were "before her time." I explained the significance of the cups.

We stopped, as I stood for several minutes analyzing the wall of cups. A few recognizable signatures jumped out at me. I saw cups signed by partners I'd met through my StarbucksMelody.com. One cup was signed by a Texas store partner, who in 2011 had been a shift supervisor. Today, he's a store manager. I knew that in April 2011 he'd taken a trip to Seattle to get closer to the brand and to join in the Global Month of Service. I saw the signature of former Canadian store partner, who by 2013, had left Starbucks. And then there was a cup of yet another store partner I knew who had been an Assistant Store Manager when he signed the cup. He's currently a store manager.

"Can I take a picture of the wall of cups?" I asked.

"Sure," my host said. I told her the story of the Starbucks fortieth anniversary events as I took photos with my phone.

In that moment of being a Starbucks storyteller, I realized that Starbucks has to constantly retell their own story. I felt privileged to be a part of that, albeit in a small way. Starbucks can tell their own story far better than one customer in Seattle, but through the StarbucksMelody.com blog, I was sharing in the job of telling the Starbucks story.

The Starbucks story comes from a Grande cup full of promise and dedication.

Chapter Sixteen: July 5, 2011

As most Seattleites know, every July 4th, thousands of people crowd into Gas Works Park for a good view of fireworks over Lake Union. And on July 5th, the park is a mess.

Every year on July 5th, Starbucks volunteers clean up the mess left behind at the park and in the surrounding neighborhood. July 5th 2011, I took the day off from work, joined a few friendly Seattle store managers, and picked up litter. The actual hard work part of the day wasn't all that fun, but I don't think picking up litter is ever intended to be fun. We had Pike Place Roast coffee beforehand and Starbucks bistro boxes for lunch afterwards.

Tori, the store manager of the Columbia Tower Starbucks, and I headed off together with heavy work gloves, and two different plastic bags. We were supposed to sort recyclables from trash. For a couple of hours, we canvassed the neighborhood area adjacent to Gas Works Park. I picked up empty beer cans, soda bottles, and empty junk food packaging. We worked as a team, one of us carrying the blue sacks indicating recyclables and the other with the clear trash bag.

When our area was looking pretty good and others were heading back to the park for the Bistro Box lunch, we walked back to the grassy lawn where a Starbucks tent was set up. The cleanup work had gone very quickly due to the large turnout of volunteers.

It was bright and sunny that day with weather in the mid-70s. It was perfect out. When Tori and I reached the designated lunch area at the park, we were intercepted by Cliff and Andrew Fried. Both were returning to the Starbucks tent at the same time that we were. I watched them. They were two men who had clearly worked up a sweat. They took picking up litter quite seriously. They each carried full and bulging bags of garbage. They put me and my half-full bag to shame.

"I think I've underperformed here," I said to Cliff, lifting up my half-full plastic sack of garbage.

Tori had already picked up her Starbucks Bistro Box and canned Refresher. She walked away, signaling for me to catch up with her.

Cliff and Andrew smiled and thanked me for helping out. I cut the conversation short. "My lunch date is calling for me," I said, pointing in the direction of Tori, who was now quite a distance away from us. They probably didn't even see whom I was pointing at. "Hey, you guys should come visit the Columbia Tower Starbucks more often. It has a great store manager!" That comment probably sounded out of the blue to them, but it wasn't to me since I'd been picking up litter with Tori.

I meant it. Tori had been part of my Starbucks world for years. Her store is the closest Starbucks to Seattle Municipal Court with a Clover coffee brewer so she had seen a lot of me over the years.

I again motioned that I had to go, feeling as though I'd abruptly ended a conversation with the *President of Just About Everything Starbucks* and Andrew Fried.

When I caught up with Tori, she leaned into me and said, "Hey, you know those two got here before we did? They had quite a head start in picking up trash."

I told her matter-of-factly what was on my mind. "I think it's amazing that Starbucks is the kind of the company where it doesn't matter if you're a top executive like Cliff or a brand-new barista, you pick up litter."

We sat on a grassy lawn, soaking up the sun, eating our lunch, and making small talk. Nearby, another store partner had overheard our conversation and chimed in. I recognized her face but didn't know her name. She'd once worked at the First and Walker Starbucks which is only a few blocks away from the Starbucks headquarters. The familiar face volunteered her story.

"Cliff used to make me so nervous. He'd come into First and Walker now and then. I got butterflies in my stomach for a long time when I saw him standing in the line. After several trips, it occurred to me that he's a nice guy like many others but for a short while, I thought I might vomit when he ordered and I was on register."

She paused her story only long enough to take another bite from her chicken and hummus Starbucks Bistro Box. "I think that it took a few times for me to see that like anyone else, he wants a good experience and a great drink."

Tori and the other Starbucks partner continued to chat. They were talking about Refreshers, food, the beautiful weather, and whatever came to mind.

As the two of them carried on, I thought back to another volunteering event, earlier in the year.

April 30, 2011, was a big day for Starbucks partners in Seattle. There had been a marquee event planned at a South Seattle neighborhood school. There were a number of cities, both in the U.S. and internationally, with big volunteering events organized by Starbucks. In Seattle, more than six hundred people turned out, both Starbucks partners and customers. There was an initial rally with speeches from Cliff Burrows, Andrew and his famous southern drawl, a few others, and the then-city mayor Mike McGinn. There were nearby locations for weeding, painting, and park cleanup.

On that April 30th, when I arrived on site, there were Starbucks partners carrying signs with numbers on them. This was how Starbucks sorted people into smaller groups. I saw Collin Longacre carrying a sign that said "14" on it. I promptly went up to him and asked him what it meant.

"Melody, if you want to be in the group doing outdoor painting, go sign up for that and you'll be in group number 14 – my group! We've got the best project! Go sign up for group 14!"

I did as instructed. I never even looked at any of the other options. I wanted to be in Collin's group.

Group 14 stayed on site at the initial school meet-up location while others drove off or walked off to other locations.

We were directed to an area of large, stacked wood panels which had to be painted. They were to be used later on as part of a refurbishment of the Fairmount Park Elementary School in West Seattle[26].

We were told to paint the tall stack of wood panels in bright colors. We could even do pretty artwork on them if we wanted. We split up into teams of three people per wood panel. I happened to be standing near two other customers-a married couple–who needed a third body. They immediately pulled me in with them, perhaps hoping I had some artistic ability. We grabbed a wood panel, and then looked for an open spot on the large playground which served as the painting area. I tried to take our panel to an area away from the main paths of foot traffic, but the married couple wanted to plop down close to the paint supplies. Out voted two-to-one, I gave in, and we plopped our wood panel down and got to work.

---

26   West Seattle is part of the city of Seattle, but many Seattleites, myself included, think that it feels like its own separate city, since it's a little isolated from the rest of Seattle, and you have to drive over the West Seattle Bridge to get to it.

I looked over, and lo and behold, the group immediately adjacent to me was Cliff, Andrew Fried, and one another person whom I didn't know. Cliff and Andrew were on their hands and knees painting wood panels. No such thing as lip service to community service for those two.

That beautiful April day, I had stopped by a South Seattle Starbucks which has some famous Martin Luther King Jr. words in wrought iron on its exterior.

"Life's most persistent and urgent question is 'What are you doing for others?'"

"Hey Melody! We're going to get going now." Tori abruptly jolted me back to reality.

"I'll walk back with you," I replied. I knew she had an apartment in the Gas Works Park neighborhood.

We headed back and I thanked her for picking up trash with me. I'd be trash buddies with her anytime.

Connect with one another, with the company, with your community.

Chapter Seventeen: I'm Not Going to Tell You That

All I could think was, "Thank God it's Friday." I was at my desk, as there is almost never any court in session on a Friday afternoon. My email dinged and I opened up a message from Mallory. "Invitation to Madison Park Store Celebration Tonight."

The Madison Park celebration party was scheduled from 4 PM to 6 PM. I walked in to find many familiar faces, all here for a big celebration of the store's remodel. The store had also added beer and wine to the menu, making it one of the few Evenings Starbucks.

I hung out with a partner named Lisa and one of her coworkers. Lisa used to be a store manager in downtown Seattle, and in 2010 she was promoted to the SSC. I missed seeing her in the stores. I easily connected with her. We talked for quite a while that night, and I mentioned that I had thought about writing a book.

"Why don't you call it *The Other Onward*?" she joked. "It sounds like your book would cover the same time in Starbucks history as Howard's *Onward* book!" She was mostly joking around but there was a hint of truth in what she was saying. I was mentally writing the customer experience of the Starbucks transformation during the *Onward* years.

I laughed at that. "I am pretty sure the title *Onward* is already taken," I said.

"What's so funny over here?" Andrew Fried walked up to our small circle.

"Hey guess what? Melody is writing *The Other Onward*." Lisa gushed.

Andrew laughed too but the expression on his face was pretty clear. "Am I going to end up a character in this book?"

"Andrew, don't worry the book isn't even written yet. But yes of course you'll get to be a character in the book." He took it in stride. "Oooh nooo," Andrew said in a teasing tone of voice.

I rambled on a little about the book. It pretty much lived in my dreams at that point, though from then on I'd secretly think of it as *The Other Onward*. I tried to explain that it would be my own stories and my own experiences. Andrew was encouraging. "I think you should write a book, Melody."

Pretty soon someone else was calling out Andrew's name, vying for his attention. The loud music of a local band continued and made normal conversation difficult. I mingled from group to group, as Andrew and others did too. Even Starbucks parties are an exercise of circling around a room and talking a loud volume over the noise of the room: competing conversations, baristas at work, and a live band.

As I approached the Madison Street entrance[27] to this store, I ran into a Starbucks Regional Director, Paul Bianchi. "I'm glad you made it Melody!" he said. Paul introduced me to a tall light-skinned African American gentleman. I had no idea who he was. To this day, I don't remember his name.

"You're Melody," asked the guy I just met, as if he hadn't heard it correctly.

"Yes, I'm Melody." *Perhaps I should whip out my Washington State Driver's License*, I thought.

---

27   The store has two entrances. A front door on a smaller side street, and a side door facing busy Madison Street .

"You're Melody?" he asked again, with more emphasis on my name this time.

"Yes, I'm Melody." I was repeating myself, totally confused.

"You're the bomb!"

He got even louder. "You're the bomb," he said as if everything should be said twice.

I froze. I was as stunned and speechless as that day that Howard caught me off guard in the Starbucks Coffee Gear Store, clutching Starbucks pens in each hand. I had no idea how to respond to this declaration. Should I confirm that yes, I was, indeed, the bomb? Or should I just thank him and excuse myself?

Paul needed to leave and so I chose the latter option and moved away. After that, it felt like the party was over for me. Isn't there some truth to the idea that one should always leave on a high note? I had made an appearance and enjoyed catching up with friends and acquaintances.

That evening, I looked at the photos from the event on my camera. I deleted nearly all of them. All I'd managed to capture was a crowded store. I had really wanted to show off the store's new look – not a party of overly caffeinated customers. I knew that I would have to return when the store was empty to get some good pictures. Most of those party-goers didn't want to be all over StarbucksMelody.com.

I vowed to go back the next morning before 7:00 AM to get photos of the empty store.

I arrived at 6:30 AM the next day. The store now looked deserted compared to when I'd seen it in party-mode the night before. The store was clean and beautiful and there was no evidence of the crowds, beer, wine, and coffee. I took tons of photos of the newly-designed Madison Park store, and ordered a Clover-brewed cup of coffee.

I was hanging out at the store when Cliff walked in. He ordered coffee and an oatmeal. I told him how I liked the store's new look and how much fun I'd had the night before. Both Cliff and Howard were at the party the previous night, though I hadn't talked much to either of them.

We chatted for a minute. At that point in Starbucks history, a store that offered beer and wine was still a very rare Starbucks. He was proud of the store's new design.

"Hey Cliff, where's the next beer and wine Starbucks going to be?" Before he replied, I threw out suggestions. "San Francisco? Denver?" I had no particular reason to pick those cities other than my belief that beer and wine would do well in an urban Starbucks. I'd lived in San Francisco during law school and from my experiences there, I thought people in San Francisco would like a beer and wine Starbucks.

This concept of Evenings stores was kind of cool, and I really did think it would be fun to know where the next one would be.

"Melody," his British accented voice trailed off. There was a long pause. And then he smiled and said, "I'm not ready to tell you that."

That was the straight-shooter answer. Of course, he wouldn't tell me where the next beer and wine Starbucks would be before an official public announcement. He wouldn't tell me any secrets. I didn't push.

I explained that I had come back to get some pictures of the store when it was empty. I thanked him for his time and took a few more photos.

Sometimes you can't do business without a few secrets.

Chapter Eighteen: It's a Bad Dream

It was September 2011. I woke up with a start from a bad dream. It had seemed so real. I was sure that my friend Minori had lost his battle with cancer. How would I even know? He was in Kyoto, and I was in Seattle.

I dreamt I had been at his funeral. It was a sunny outdoor funeral. I was lost and confused. I didn't hear words that made sense. I don't speak Japanese, but what I heard was the kind of nonsense sometimes heard in cartoons like when the adults and teachers speak to Linus and Charlie Brown. But it was clear it was a funeral. I was dressed in all black. I felt a tidal wave of grief. It was just a dream. Wasn't it?

I immediately fired up my computer and went to Twitter. I tweeted at him right away. I simply told him that I panicked and had a nightmare that he had passed on. It was short and blunt, but since you're limited to 140 characters on Twitter, lots of things come out being a little blunter than intended.

It took seven long days for Minori to tweet back at me. Seven long days. I worked as usual and thought of him. I made coffee in the morning and thought of him. Maybe he had really died.

You can't imagine my relief when the reply tweet came. Much later in emails, I learned that he indeed had been in the hospital again. But he was very much alive.

@SbuxMel You will receive e-mail from my friend within a few days when I die. In other words I'm not dead when you don't get that.

He's going to be fine. He'll get to take another trip to Seattle, and have another chance to meet Howard Schultz, I thought. He had said over and over again that he dreamed of meeting Howard. I was reassured by the tweet. It was a good sign that he was back on Twitter.

Almost two years had gone by since his last attempt at meeting Howard Schultz. He was on a mission. On December 10, 2009, the Coffee City Blog of the Seattle Times[28] wrote this about Minori:

A Japanese importer and exporter of car parts, he vacations in Seattle to bask in its abundance of Starbucks. Five years ago, he visited 100 stores between here and Olympia and tried to meet Howard Schultz. Minori even has the Starbucks headquarters name tag to prove it, but says he never shook Schultz's hand.

He arrived in Seattle yesterday for a three-week visit in which he wants to pack as many stores as possible...

For an ordinary customer, trying to meet Howard Schultz is like trying to schedule some of the President's time. Perhaps a determined person can do it, but it's even more challenging if you live across the Pacific. Howard has a billion dollar corporation to run and probably, as harsh as it is to say, doesn't have time to worry about individual fans here and there, no matter who they are.

My confidence that everything was going to fine was pretty short lived. In December that year, out of the blue, I got an email from Minori.

How are you?

I hope you are doing well.

---

28   http://seattletimes.com/html/coffeecity/2010476549_starbucks_customer_from_japan.html

I continue still fighting against a cancer. It was November of the last year that I underwent surgery. So, one year passes from that. My fight will still continue, I think…

"Give me health". I ask so Santa Claus now. Haha.

I cannot travel because I am not well-conditioned. Many friends encouraged me, but I cannot visit Seattle at this end of the year. My physical strength has considerably decreased. I do not have even physical strength to go to Starbucks, but your blog makes me happy.

I want to become healthy. And I want to drink coffee with you again in Starbucks.

Thank you.
Minori

I wanted to cry. *He's a strong fighter. He will be okay*, I told myself. I replied back with how much I cared and worried, and that I believed he would be fine.

On December 4, 2011, I ran an article about him and encouraged my readers to send him speedy recovery wishes and prayers, and to send an ecard from Starbucks.com. That year, the Starbucks website had a selection of holiday ecards that customers could send to one another. The link – long since gone – was http://www.starbucks.com/merry.

On December 7th, Minori tweeted that many people had sent him ecards. His email was overflowing with mail from merry@Starbucks.com.

Thank you very much to http://starbucksmelody.com readers! Thank you for encouragement, and thank you for big love! http://twitpic.com/7q2igl

Holidays came and went. The red cup season at Starbucks came and went. I only heard from him a few more times. A couple of emails telling me that he was in and out of a Kyoto hospital. Christmas Blend season came and went. Of course, all I could do was act normal. The Seattle rains came and went.

No matter what I was doing, in the back of my mind, I wondered how Minori was holding up. I was hoping not to get that email from his friend, "within a few days when I die."

Chapter Nineteen: Blonde Roast

In September 2011, I got an email from Mallory. "We'd like to invite you to the headquarters . . . but it's a big secret." A flurry of emails followed. Would I be willing to sign a non-disclosure agreement? I hadn't signed an NDA before. The lawyer in me wondered if I could create exceptions so that I'd have a couple of store partners to bounce ideas off of when this secret event – whatever it was – was over. In the end, I didn't have negotiation power. I still wanted to experience whatever this big secret was. If I was going to go to this event, whatever it was, it would be on their terms. I agreed.

On that day in early September, I went to the Starbucks headquarters as usual, taking the light rail from Pioneer Square to SODO, and walking down Lander Street to the headquarters. I met up with Mallory and she introduced me to her colleague, Nate. We were escorted down a winding hallway with conference rooms and rooms showing off store designs.

We entered a room called the "Tea Tasting Room." This is not how I had pictured a tea tasting room. The room was a busy, jumble of objects and didn't scream "tea" to me. If you're caught consuming a Diet Coke in that room, do the keepers of the Tea Tasting Room kick you out? It was a small 8 x 10 room, with a tall, narrow table for four to six, and a few shelves with decorative and ornate tins, tea pots, and jars. A box lantern hung from the ceiling. The room was intimate, cozy, and somehow made me think of a small room in an upscale Chinese restaurant, not a corporate tea tasting room. There was a lot going on in this room. Green aprons hung crowded on hooks. On one shelf, I recognized a Jebena pottery vessel. A Jebena is a special pottery jar used for serving Ethiopian coffee.

I settled on a tall chair in corner of the mis-named Tea Tasting Room with a view out a window staring at a sea of white cubicles and waist-high partitions. The contrast between this warm and inviting room and the long rows of cubicles was absolutely striking. The room looked like an oasis in the sterile corporate office.

Eugen set up several French presses of coffee, and there were whole bean coffee bags on this table that I didn't recognize. "We're going to introduce you to Blonde Roast." Eugen explained further. "It's an all new coffee and you're trying it very early."

I was confused.

Mallory added to Eugen's coffee explanation. "It's a whole new coffee category – and you're one of the first to know! We haven't told our store partners yet!"

I was trying hard to feign excitement. Turns out, some people want a thin mouth-feel, weak coffee. I'm not one of them. I want my coffee to be coffee, and my tea to be tea, and never the twain shall meet.

Mallory was still bubbling with excitement. "And look the packaging is all new! Customers will love the simplified, easier to understand packaging." She is PR through and through.

By simplified, did Starbucks mean dull?

I'd already signed that damn Non-Disclosure Agreement. It was too late to run from this coffee tasting in the Tea Tasting Room.

I suck at lying. I have one of those faces where my every emotion is right there for everyone to see. I hate that. I assume that even in the world of coffee, at times a poker face is of great value. "Yes, I love this coffee,"

I said through clenched teeth.

"Oh I love the new packaging[29]! It's so clean!" I was lying through my teeth. I hated it. It did nothing to tell the story of the coffee. It was boring. Did the Starbucks partners know I didn't like it? If I told the truth, would I ever be invited back again? I wanted coffee packaging that had some romance of the bean to it. The packaging should look as lovingly made as the painstaking hours it took for farmers to pick coffee cherries from coffee trees, one by one. It should not have a simple two color label with a small icon for the coffee, divorced from the aroma, taste, and story of the bean.

Eugen poured some of the new coffees, and explained that Starbucks tried eighty recipes of blends of various Latin American beans to arrive at the all-new Veranda Blend. *Oh God, it's watery. What the heck am I going to say on the blog? These corporate partners are trying so hard.*

Next, we tried the new Willow Blend, an African bean blend, again roasted to a tea-like profile. *Please, can we eeek out a wee bit more caramelization to these beans? It never has to be taken to an Italian or French Roast extreme, but a nice light-medium roast profile like Breakfast Blend is fine.*

As a coffee is roasted, its acidity is lowered, and sweetness increases by the process of the natural sugars in the coffee caramelizing. From my cherished Starbucks Coffee Master training book, which was given to me as a gift for being a passionate customer, I knew a little bit about roasting.

"We roast green coffee beans to draw out their aroma, acidity, body

---

29   That version of whole bean coffee packaging was short lived. It was phased in during 2012. By the summer of 2013, it was being phased out for more lively coffee packaging. I can only assume that Starbucks too eventually decided that it didn't work.

and flavor. The intense heat of the roasting process triggers a complex chemical reaction within the beans. Sugars and starches in green coffee beans are transformed into the precious oils that give our coffee much of its rich flavor and aroma. The longer a coffee bean is roasted, the more these oils develop. At the same time, moisture is drawn out of the beans.

... As each bean loses its moisture, it "pops." A chemical reaction called pyrolysis takes place – starches convert into sugars, proteins disintegrate and the entire cellular structure of the bean is altered.

...The second pop, toward the end of the roast, is the most critical stage of roasting..." [30]

"This Willow Blend will be really amazing iced!" I could say that easily with a straight face. A lot of East African blends of coffees work well when iced. We did some comparing and contrasting of the new blonde coffees with Pike Place Roast and Italian Roast. Regardless of what I thought of the coffees, this kind of coffee tasting - with true masters at the headquarters - was an incredibly valuable experience. I remember one coffee master years ago – and a person who helped author the current Starbucks coffee master book - say to me "compare and contrast, compare and contrast: that's how you learn about coffee."

I walked out of the Tea Tasting Room bewildered. At least I had more than a month to think about what I might write on this experience. Because of the terms of that tiny-print Non-Disclosure Agreement, I wasn't going to be able to write on the new – I mean boring – packaging and two watery coffees until Starbucks gave me the green light, or maybe the Blonde Light.

I jotted down a draft of a blog article right away. I wanted to get thoughts down while still fresh in my mind. This is what I wrote:

---

30   *Starbucks Coffee Master Journal*, 2010, p.78

I thought the Veranda Blend was a little boring. It reminded me a bit of drinking a Level 1 or Level 2 Seattle's Best Coffee. Nonetheless, I have a feeling that Veranda is going to have its big fans. It is a taste profile that many Americans know and love: the distinctive acidity and bright flavor of a washed Latin American coffee.

I had two choices. I could be honest. Or I could lie. It boiled down to that. To call Veranda "boring" was a truer statement than to say I was a fan of it. Perhaps it was a gentle statement, but I couldn't say that I loved something that I didn't. Whether or not I loved it didn't matter. This coffee would still have its fans.

Perhaps this explains why many Fortune 500 corporations are a little thin on the whole "Customer Outreach" thing. It's much nicer *not* to hear your fans criticize you.

I will always say things that make people mad, I reminded myself, as I continued to type a draft post. In the larger scheme of things, you cannot create a blog that some people love without disappointing, angering, or annoying a few people now and then.

I settled firmly on "boring" as the right word for Veranda Blend. Coffee taste is so extremely subjective. It will still end up being someone's favorite. I crossed my fingers that I would be invited back to the headquarters again for another chance at a fun event, despite this instance of failed "Customer/Blogger Outreach."

Starbucks doesn't care what I write about them, I thought. They realize they don't pay me, and they know that not every story I write will be positive. *My blog is too small to have any impact on a billion dollar corporation.* I felt sure of this. Over the course of years of articles and comments, some will anger, some will disappoint, some will bring smiles, and some will vex. I mentally swung back and forth, one minute thinking what I write is important to Starbucks, and the next minute reminding myself that I'm a very small fish in a sea of coffee. I stopped worrying about it. I would write whatever I wanted.

I did eventually ask Mallory why they took the time to allow me to preview the Blonde Roast coffees so much earlier than the rest of the world.

"Well we thought it would be good if you were ready to field questions on the new coffees. Some people will end up turning to you for questions."

I wrote my blog article about the Blonde Roast Coffees and forgot about it for a while. About a month went by before I got the Blonde Light to go ahead and publish. And I did. And again, I didn't think much about it. The coffee wouldn't be released nationwide until January 2012, so for most every customer, there was no way to go try the coffee . . . yet.

The weeks flew by, and if you were to count time in cups of coffee, the seasons of Anniversary Blend, Thanksgiving Blend, and Christmas Blend came and went faster than one could imagine. One moment there was the red packaging of Christmas Blend with pointy-nosed characters looking up to the sky making wishes, and then it was all gone, as quickly as it came.

And then came January 2012. Starbucks launched and heavily promoted their two new coffees, complete with in-store sampling and sample size packages of beans.

On January 10, 2012, the Seattle Times wrote about the new Blonde roasts. The journalists must've been reading StarbucksMelody.com. I felt like I was going to throw up a little. My word "boring" would forever be memorialized in the Seattle Times[31].

An early Seattle taster, blogger Melody Overton, reported that while

31   http://blogs.seattletimes.com/allyoucaneat/2012/01/10/starbucks_starts_offering_ligh/

she's a fan of bolder coffees … She found the Veranda boring, but predicted it would win fans anyway.

I reminded myself that I'd had two choices. I could say I was a fan of the coffee, or not. Simple as that. *Better to have some credibility and say that you don't like something*, I assured myself, as I drank the annual seasonal favorite coffee, Casi Cielo. Each January, Starbucks offers this delicious medium roast coffee of fine Guatemala Antigua coffee beans. It was a good way to start the year, and not think about Blonde Roast blunders[32].

I thought for sure that I would never again get to grace the inside of the SSC, and that maybe a few partners inside the headquarters were sorely disappointed in my choice of adjectives for Veranda Blend.

Eventually, I stopped worrying. An ethics professor at U.C. Hastings College of the Law had always pounded into our head one thing.

Credibility is the currency we trade on.

---

32   Over time, Veranda Blend did eventually grow on me. It will never be a favorite coffee or my "go to" coffee, but I slowly grew to appreciate it.

Chapter Twenty: The Smith Tower Closes

The Smith Tower closed its doors forever in early February 2012. There aren't many urban Seattle Starbucks stores that don't make it. This one was so slow and so unprofitable that Starbucks shut it down.

To me, it was a big loss. It was the closest Starbucks to my office – no more than a tenth of a mile away. It wasn't the store that I visited most, but it had huge sentimental value to me.

By that year, most of my colleagues realized that I had a strong interest in Starbucks. On a regular basis, colleagues would swing by my office at work to tell me their thoughts on Starbucks. I heard it all: their feedback on stores, their ideas for new drinks and products, and I got to see a lot of favorite coffee mugs. Universally, my colleagues loved the Smith Tower Starbucks.

I got used to this odd dynamic. Peter, a senior attorney, would tell me that the Smith Tower had the best espresso shots. Holly would tell me that she was upset that some stores refused to steam lemonade. Carolina was adamant that every coffee tumbler should have big sturdy handles. Another colleague wanted Starbucks to bring back almond syrup.

But the most touching words always came from my boss – the attorney who wrote my performance reviews. "You know Melody, Callie and I go for a Starbucks run every Thursday morning. The Smith Tower partners are always so polite and kind with her." This ritual was important to both of them.

Callie is a developmentally-delayed adult with mild autism. She's worked in our office for many years doing basic tasks and everyone loves her. She's bright and kind, but has a child's view of the world in many ways.

One day my boss and I discussed some of the other Starbucks in the area.

"What about the one on the corner of First and Yesler?" I asked.

"No. I don't like that one. I always seem to run into clients there." Though no fault of Starbucks, Pioneer Square evolved and deteriorated over the years and the walk down Yesler often revealed open drug use, panhandling, and people sleeping on the sidewalk.

I threw out more suggestions. "What about the Starbucks in the Washington Shoe Building?" The Washington Shoe building is a historic building over 100 years old on South Jackson Street, about a third of a mile from our office.

"No, I'm not a fan of that one either. I don't like the vibe in there."

Finally, he settled on the Fourth and Cherry Starbucks. They were always patient with Callie, though she still preferred the Smith Tower location.

One day, not long after that conversation, the Smith Tower closed. That store held many memories for me. It was where I first met Collin Longacre. It was where I first discovered that Starbucks was more than just a company that sold coffee. And it was the store that helped my colleagues share and understand my passion for Starbucks. To this day, Collin remains one of my favorite partners and Callie still talks about how nice everyone was to her. I still wander by the Smith Tower sometimes and get a little wistful.

You never know when your kindness can change someone's life.

Chapter Twenty-One: April Fool's Day 2012

April 1, 2012 was a Sunday. I got up early. This isn't natural for me, but the day before I'd arrived home after a vacation to Boston to see my sister. I think I was still on East Coast time.

I started my day with a walk to the original Starbucks at 1912 Pike Place. I wanted to see the friendly store manager, who had been the recipient of gifts from Minori, including a Japan Bearista bear, which sat on display on a shelf in that store.

The store manager wasn't in on this early Sunday morning. I ordered a Tall Vanilla Latte, bought a couple of small merchandise items exclusive to that store, and chatted for a few minutes with the barista working the bar. Many people don't know that the 1912 Pike Place Starbucks is the only United States store using a La Marzocco espresso machine. It's a high quality manual espresso maker. At one time, every Starbucks was equipped with a La Marzocco. Eventually, the La Marzocco brand espresso machines were pulled out of every United States Starbucks, as it no longer met Starbucks' demands of speed of service and consistency of espresso shot. In addition, with the La Marzocco, Starbucks felt as though there was a risk repetitive motion injuries due to the strain of pulling manual espresso shots in a high volume café setting. Because 1912 Pike Place is a historic Starbucks, one of several unique things about it is that it has retained its La Marzocco espresso machine.

I overheard a customer say that she was visiting all the way from Florida to see this store. I shouldn't be surprised when I hear this, but I still am. People travel from all over the world to visit the Starbucks "where it all began."

"That's a really long distance to come to Starbucks!" I said this despite the fact that I too would travel to visit a Starbucks. In fact, I had to admit that I had done exactly that. "But, I would totally do the same, and I've even traveled to a few cities to write about Starbucks stores for a blog that I produce called StarbucksMelody."

"You're StarbucksMelody?" came the loud and surprised response. "I read your blog all the time!" That reaction still weirds me out a bit.

"Hey, can I get my picture taken with you?" the Florida customer asked. As it turns out, she's a shift supervisor in a small café-only Florida Starbucks.

Regardless of how I felt about pictures, it seemed like the right thing to do at the moment. We chatted for a few more minutes and then I left 1912 Pike Place. I was hungry, and that Starbucks doesn't sell food.

Sometimes tourists arrive at the historic 1912 Pike Place Starbucks and are a little disappointed that there is no food at all at that store. I believe it is the only Starbucks with no food whatsoever. The original lease forbade Starbucks from selling newspapers or any baked food items inside 1912 Pike Place Starbucks. The Market didn't want Starbucks competing with the large variety of food offered at other vendors and there was already a large newspaper stand about two blocks away. Starbucks Coffee Company, which at that time sold only loose leaf tea, spices, and coffee, willingly signed the lease with the non-compete agreement. In the early 1970s, the owners of Starbucks didn't anticipate any need to ever offer food inside their then-two Starbucks stores: 1912 Pike Place and a store in Seattle's University Village. To this day, Starbucks willingly renews that lease with the non-compete agreement. Not even a pre-baked Madeleine cookie pre-wrapped in plastic is allowed to be sold. It would violate the agreement.

Thinking about a light breakfast and coffee, I walked up to Starbucks at Fourth and Union. I really liked this store's manager too, and I hoped I would see her, even though I knew that the odds were slim. It seems as though Sundays are the days one is least likely to find a Starbucks store manager in his or her store.

The morning was as ordinary as can be. The store was pretty quiet. I ordered a Chonga bagel[33] and a Clover–brewed cup of Sumatra, and sat down with my phone, ready for a few games of Words With Friends. I took off my glasses so I could see my phone. *Damn it Melody. You really do need bifocals.*

I was pretty engrossed in food and coffee, and not even making small talk with the two very nice baristas working that morning. I looked up. Was that Howard Schultz at the register? Yes it was. He was dressed in jeans, a button down shirt, and a baseball cap. He seemed to be having a lazy Sunday morning too.

In that moment, it felt like he had invaded *my* Starbucks. I was here first. I pinched myself. This wasn't a store that I would expect him to drop by. It didn't stand out as a flagship high profile store quite the way that East Olive Way or some other Seattle Starbucks stores do.

Starbucks operates a few stores which stand out of the many thousands because they're "high profile" stores. Because these stores are more visible, they're more likely to get executive visits to ensure that all is in order. A high profile Starbucks store is destination Starbucks, for one reason or another. It may have a cutting edge store design. It may serve beer and wine. It may have an especially desirable location in its city,

---

33   The Chonga Bagel is a Pacific Northwest favorite and a regional Starbucks offering. It's a CHeese ONion GArlic bagel.

attracting people to visit it. Those characteristics may add up to a store being a high profile store. The Starbucks at East Olive Way fits this description: It has a one of kind store design, a Clover coffee brewer, and offers beer and wine.

The Fourth and Union Starbucks is a very nice store, but not really a high profile one. I was *sure* that Howard was invading my store.

Howard saw me, though he was still lingering at the register. I came up to him, and prodded him. "Hey, remember you still owe me a little coffee meeting?" Only a few weeks had gone by since the March 2012 annual meeting of shareholders. I'd caught up with Howard immediately after the meeting was over and asked, "Can we sit down and chat over a French press?" Little did he know, I had no particular agenda in mind but genuinely thought it would be fun to have coffee with him. His reply was resoundingly positive. "Yes. We'll make that happen." He could've easily provided a much more ambiguous answer. I was following up on that conversation from a few weeks earlier.

"Yes, of course, Melody. We will make that happen. We will." He sounded 100% sincere. I didn't have any reason to doubt him. I figured it would eventually happen. I had no pressing schedule and he knew how to find me.

Together, we drifted in the direction of the beverage pick-up bar area. The conversation continued. I mentioned to him that I was planning to see the newly-remodeled Magnolia Starbucks later that day. He seemed talkative. "Hey, have you seen the Green Lake store's remodel? What did you think?" Howard asked.

I was flattered that Howard Schultz even considered what I thought of a major store remodel. It was probably polite small talk but trust me, I will indulge Howard Schultz.

"Oh, I liked it." And then I chided him. "Howard, you're clearly not reading my blog! I wrote a review of that store!"

Howard laughed. I had caught him off guard. He leaned into me, "Melody, how many people *are* reading your blog?" I cannot think of a smarter segue into a question about my blog's analytics. I was nervous. Anything I said could be held against me, and expectations like that are hard to live up to. "Oh, it's about 30,000 unique visitors a month." I low-balled a number at him, as nervous as heck that I'd be forever setting a bar that I needed to live up to in the eyes of the world of Starbucks.

As I write this in January 2014, the blog receives just under 80,000 unique visitors a month. But it goes up and down.

I rather abruptly changed the topic. "Hey Howard! Can I take your picture?" Taking a picture is like documenting that something really happened, and it wasn't a dream. I really was thinking that it would be the coolest thing ever to tweet this moment and say I chatted with Howard Schultz at the Fourth & Union Starbucks! I knew I had Twitter followers who would be oh-so-jealous.

He looked at me and simply said, "Nooo." It was a long, drawn out, and tired no. It really seemed to say, "I'm tired of having my photo taken all the time," though I have no idea what he was really thinking. I had to respect the simplicity of his no. "Oh, okay," I replied.

His short latte came up at the bar. I headed back down to my table, staring at a now cold, half-eaten bagel with cream cheese. Howard headed out of the store, sipping his short non-fat latte as he went. He stopped right at my table. And in a moment of clearly reading my mind, as he saw me sitting there fiddling with my phone, he said to me, "Hey Melody, no tweeting this!"

I had to laugh. Howard Schultz knew me. And so I didn't. I was perfectly tight-lipped about the nice conversation at Fourth & Union Starbucks.

Long after Howard left, the barista, Chuck, came up to my table. He had a look of wonder on his face. "I didn't know who that was!" It took me a minute to process his words. It didn't occur to me that any downtown Seattle Starbucks baristas might not recognize Howard Schultz. "You didn't recognize Howard?"

He shook his head. "I had never met him before." I could tell he needed to get back to his post. He was turning his head furtively at the empty register. But before he darted off, he said, "When you went up to him to talk to him, by the tone of the conversation you had, I assumed that he must have been one of your lawyer friends. Later on it struck me that that's Howard."

I had to laugh. The whole thing struck me as funny. Howard as a lawyer?

I summed up some of the Howard lessons I'd learned over time. "Howie" is a huge no-no. He's not fond of having his photo taken early on a Sunday morning. I already knew that Howard Schultz was nowhere to be found on social media. It was likely he wasn't a fan of social media at all.

At the end of the day, I simply enjoyed another opportunity to talk about Starbucks with Howard and wished that Minori would have that chance too.

Not every experience needs to be epic to be memorable.

Chapter Twenty-Two: Good Bye

On April 17, 2012, I received the following email message.

日々みなさまには温かいご教示を頂いておりましたが、
このたび天寿を全うすることとなり、
以前よりお願いしていた友人の協力を得て、
こうしてみなさまへの告知をさせて頂いております。
２０１０年より闘病を続けておりましたが真にお恥ずかしい話で、
ガンという病に負ける形となってしまいました。
何の恩返しもできないまま他界してしまったことにはただ悔しさを覚えるばかりでござ
いますが、
皆様のご健康とより一層のご発展をお祈り申し上げます。
突然のお報せ、そして拙い文章でのご無礼不調法はご容赦くださいませ。

皆様と知合えた感謝の念、そしてご恩は決して忘れません。ありがとうございました。

なおこのメールへの返信を頂いても、誰も読むことはありませんのでご了承ください。

To my friends. Hello, I have bad news today. My fight against illness that continued from 2010 got an ending. I lost the fight. I left this sentence to my friend to notify you when I died. So, I'm sorry. But I do not forget you. You are a very good friend. Please love your families and friends. Thank you very much.
* Please do not reply to this e-mail. Nobody can answer it.

With my late night fully-caffeinated coffee in hand, I stared at the screen and cried. Even now, I cannot re-read those words without tearing up. Minori was an amazing and sweet person who had come into my life for a few short years, all because of Starbucks. He brought lots of joy to lots of people. Each time he came to Seattle, he adorned partners with gifts from Japan. Tumblers, mugs, you name it. But the most generous gift he gave was that of himself. His friendship. I didn't have words, other than to say I missed him. Cancer snatched him up so fast. It was an indiscriminate, unfair disease.

I emailed Andrew Fried to let him know, as Minori had talked on the phone with Andrew once in the car. Within a few hours, Andrew emailed me back, and said he was sorry for my loss.

I cried some more.

I miss my friend.

Chapter Twenty-Three: When Cliff Says He'll Look Into That

My Android phone died. They have such short life spans. One Tuesday morning, I discovered that my HTC Evo was dead. I needed a new phone. By that Saturday (July 21, 2012), I was in serious phone-withdrawal mode. At least I was able to tweet now and then from my Kindle that week. I planned to be the first person in the door when the Sprint store on Union Street opened.

I started the day by dropping by Evolution Fresh and grabbing a Southwest Scramble for breakfast. Starbucks operates four Evolution Fresh juice bars across the country, two in Seattle. The Evolution Fresh stores have amazingly fresh foods, healthy items, and a huge array of fresh juice offerings.

I didn't plan my morning very well, since I didn't know what time the Sprint store opened. It turns out, it opens at 10:00 AM on Saturdays. By 9:30 AM, I was sitting in the Starbucks at 6th & Union, directly across the street from the Sprint store. I drank coffee, played Words With Friends on my Kindle, and waited impatiently for Sprint to open.

A few minutes after 10:00 AM, I walked into the Sprint store on a mission to obtain a working phone. You have no idea the phone withdrawals I had gone through that week. I was inside the Sprint store for a full hour, possibly more. The Sprint employee pointed me in the direction of the newest HTC Evo, which was the HTC Evo 4g LTE. I quickly fell in love. The helpful Sprint employee set up the new phone, showed me some of the bells and whistles, adjusted a few of the settings to my liking, and helped me pick out a sturdy case, as I'm a bit rough on my phone. We even charged the phone for a few minutes. I walked out on cloud nine, new phone in hand.

I hurried back across the street, back into the 6th and Union Starbucks. Of course, now all I could do was play with my new phone. I ordered an iced Kenya coffee from the Clover brewer, a perfect summer drink, and began to take photos and play with my new toy. I sent out my first tweet with my new phone – a photo of the store. The store wasn't all that busy while I was there.

When I write articles for StarbucksMelody.com, I like to feature vibrant Starbucks stores with the latest designs. It's not the only subject on my website, but a beautiful store often makes for an inviting and fun article. Up to this point, I hadn't covered the 6th & Union Starbucks for StarbucksMelody.com. I genuinely like the pretty, newly-remodeled Starbucks stores that have special features like a Clover coffee brewer. I snapped away furiously with my new phone, figuring that a few of the pictures could frame a nice article on this store.

I had a great time that morning chatting with some of the enthusiastic partners on the floor. I connected with Cameron, whom I met some time ago when he was a shift supervisor at 1912 Pike Place. Now he is an Assistant Store Manager at 6th & Union. He's very passionate and knowledge about Starbucks.

Customers came and went in waves. One moment the store was empty and the next moment there was a long, snaking line. While I was taking photos, the store began to pick up, with several customers walking in. I continued to have fun playing with my new phone and taking photos, paying little attention to the growing line at the register.

Cameron came up to me, and tapped on my shoulder to get me to look up from my phone. "Look! Cliff Burrows is over there," he said. "Have you met Cliff? I assume you know him?" There was a question in his voice.

"Yes, yes, Cliff and I go way back," I said jokingly. I realized that while Howard Schultz may be a household name, Cliff Burrows probably isn't as well known outside of the world of Starbucks partners. He should be. Being that I'm a Cliff fan, I joked with myself that I should work on giving him a little more publicity on StarbucksMelody.com. Full-time lawyer, part-time publicist. That's me. I wasn't seriously considering this, but the thought made me smile.

I was thankful Cameron had given me the heads up. Somehow Cliff had managed to enter the store and get in line without me noticing. Cliff also appeared to be inspecting the merchandise wall to ensure that everything was in top notch shape. I was amazed that somehow I'd been so into my phone, I'd not noticed Cliff at all. It felt a bit like a celebrity was in the room.

I left my table at a far end of the store, and approached Cliff. He immediately saw me and gave me a warm hello. We jumped right into comfortable small talk, as if we were picking up a conversation that we started a few days earlier.

Coincidentally, the day before, Starbucks opened up a new Evolution Fresh juice bar in downtown Seattle. Starbucks operates four Evolution Fresh juice bars, and the Pine Street store had its grand opening July 20, 2012.

"Have you been to the new Evolution Fresh bar?" Cliff asked.

"Cliff, I was there early in the morning as it opened. I might not have a need for a kitchen anymore. I'm going to love having juice and salads there." Maybe I should have asked him if he had a favorite juice, but I switched gears on him[34]. I was still thinking about the small number of stores that offer the exquisite Starbucks Reserve coffees brewed with the special Clover coffee brewer.

"I think there should be more Clover stores," I told Cliff. And then I made a specific request. "It would be great to have a Starbucks with a Clover brewer at the store closest to my mom's house in Orange County, California."

"I can look into that. Which store do you mean?" Cliff asked, as he pulled out a smart phone and stylus to take notes.

"I don't know the store number," I told him.

He laughed. "I wasn't expecting you to memorize store numbers."

I tried to narrow it down for him. "It's the Starbucks on Tustin Avenue." I gave him the cross street too.

"Melody, I've got plenty here to find the store. And, I *will* look into that for you." Cliff sounded sincere, but I wasn't going to hold my breath. I knew that Starbucks had to be judicious about which stores got a Clover coffee brewer. Secretly, I crossed my fingers.

When I got home, I saw that Cliff had managed to sneak into two of the photos that I took. His back is to the camera though, so he's hard to spot in the photo, unless you're looking for him.

---

34   Also in the summer of 2012, I saw Cliff at an event at the Terry and Republican Starbucks (in Seattle) for the launch of the new Evenings food. Stores that are Evenings stores not only offer beer and wine, but also elevated food offerings such as chocolate fondue, flatbreads with artichokes and goat cheese, mac and cheese, bacon wrapped dates, chicken skewers and more. I had asked Ciiff what his favorite of the new Evenings foods was. His answer? "The bacon wrapped dates." Now you know.

I didn't realize it until much later, but Cliff kept his promise about looking into whether that Starbucks in Orange County would get a Clover.

Keep your promises and you'll delight your fans.

Chapter Twenty-Four: A California Surprise

In June 2013, I took two weeks off from work and went on vacation in California. My mom and most of my siblings live in Orange County, so this is a common vacation destination for me. My mom and I have been to Disneyland countless times. On this trip, I wasn't prepared for the bright California sunshine, and I really wanted a pair of prescription sunglasses for driving. I found an optometrist at Main Place Mall, in Santa Ana, who could make me a pair quickly. It was a financial splurge, but it would make driving around much more comfortable in Orange County, and possibly in Seattle, too.

Main Place Mall is on Main Street, where the city of Orange meets Santa Ana. I decided to stop for a wonderful cold Refreshers drink at the Starbucks at the corner of Main Street and Chapman Avenue. I didn't know anyone there. In Seattle, when I walk into a Starbucks, I am often recognized by a store partner. I'm sometimes surprised that I'm not very anonymous in Seattle, though I suppose I shouldn't be. After all, I visit Starbucks frequently, partners often transfer from store to store or cover shifts at different stores, and some Starbucks partners in Seattle follow me on Twitter, Facebook, at or StarbucksMelody.com.

On this Starbucks run, I felt anonymous. I ordered my Refresher and sat down to charge my phone a bit before continuing on my way. I sat quietly on a bench, completely engrossed with my phone. After a few minutes, I was interrupted. Looking up, I observed a young man dressed in black, carrying a green apron under his left arm. It looked like he was either starting or ending his shift.

"Are you Melody?"

"Yes," I confirmed. Well, my name *was* on my cup.

"No, I mean are you that girl with the blog about Starbucks?"

Whoa. This was weird. I had no idea who this guy was. I didn't know anyone at the Starbucks store at Chapman and Main Streets in Orange. He had recognized me. My photo is on my Twitter profile and the Facebook page that I manage for my blog. Nevertheless, it felt strange to be recognized. The name on the cup must've helped, but still.

"I read your blog all the time." He pulled up a chair. "I'm Jun." We made small talk. "How did you end up starting a blog?"

Oh, if I got a dollar every time someone asks me that question, I'd be a very happy woman.

Over the years, I've tried to figure out how to answer that in a sound-bite length answer. I used to give a lengthy answer that began with "I moved to Seattle in 1989." I'd end with, "In 2006, I got a job in downtown Seattle, and in 2008, Howard Schultz returned as CEO of Starbucks and all these rapid changes began to happen around me. New coffees, Clover stores, concept stores, and more." I'd try to fill in details of the intervening years. I'd watch eyes glaze over as I related that long answer.

Even worse, a few people would ask me how I ended up in Seattle in 1989, and I'd have to explain that in 1988, when I was enlisted, the Air Force sent me to McChord AFB in Tacoma, Washington. Those "How did you start a blog conversations" could spin out of control into a long life story very quickly.

I answered the young Starbucks partner's question with a much simpler answer. "Oh well, I really thought the world needed a fun, uplifting Starbucks blog, and I got lucky that I had a bunch of unique experiences since I'm so close to the headquarters." I was quite pleased that my sound-bite answer was improving with time.

Jun broached his idea for a business venture and website. It was a couponing website focused around coffee and tea. He spelled it out for me. I was drained. Sure, I was flattered to be recognized, but over the years of blogging, I'd been sent countless random emails by unknown people who all thought they had some amazing product, blog, or idea that they thought I should feature. Jun hadn't quite figured out how to pitch his Coffee-A-Coupon website in a sound-bite. I politely took down the URL and promised him that I would look at it soon. As it turned out, this was all still in the imagination stage.

I excused myself. "Hey, I'm on vacation, and I need to head back to my mom's house." That was a true statement. I walked out incredibly flattered that I had been recognized and a little disappointed that his real interest been his sales pitch.

When my blog was brand new, I was flattered by every email and proposal that anyone sent me. But over time, some of the repeat emails wore me out. Everyone thinks they have some perfect product that relates to coffee – and many think that I can open the door for them to Starbucks, or alternatively, they hope that my website will be good PR for them. I started to immediately delete emails that contained words like *I have designed a new kind of XYZ coffee thing.* It could be a sleeve, a cup holder, a special cup, or a special coffee lid. I am not the door to a Starbucks executive in merchandising.

During this same trip to Orange County, I walked into the Starbucks on Tustin Avenue, not far from my mom's house. This was the Orange County Starbucks that I knew the very best. I walked in and caught up with the store manager, Virginia. Virginia recognized me, which was amazing to me since she sees me only about twice a year. She has an incredible memory. Those who put on a green apron seem to magically acquire the ability to accurately recall names, faces, and often drink orders, too.

Virginia said, "Oh hey, I wanted to let you know something. It was out of the blue . . . a while ago some corporate guys from Seattle came in and measured our store's bar area and crunched some numbers to see if our store could support a Clover coffee brewer. It was a while ago – maybe a whole year ago - but I remember you telling me once how you want a Clover at the store near your mom's house." Virginia's memory is super human. I was blown away that she remembered all that.

I realized then that Virginia's experience must have been Cliff Burrows' doing. Around the time she described, I'd had a conversation with Cliff at the Sixth and Union Starbucks in Seattle about this very subject. A man of his word, Cliff had clearly followed up. He always follows up, answers email, and puts his money where his mouth is. This is why he is the President of Just About Everything Starbucks. I know a bazillion partners who are in awe of Howard. But Cliff is my hero.

"What happened? Virginia, you still don't have a Clover." I was curious if the store was slated to get one of these special coffee brewers.

"It didn't work out." Virginia was disappointed. "We're a small, low volume café. We don't have the numbers or really even the size to make a Clover brewer work."

At least it had been considered. I knew that a store had to have the right volume of customers, size, and good coffee sales to make a Clover brewer work.

It didn't matter. I'd come back to this store over and over again.

Heroes always follow through.

Chapter Twenty-Five: Callie and the Bearista Bear

It was January 2013. Callie came by my office one morning, as I sat quietly staring at my computer, trying to get through a few emails. My door was wide open, as it always is.

Callie mumbled something that I didn't quite catch. She doesn't always speak clearly. Her disability and delayed development can make her a bit hard to understand if you're not paying attention.

Even worse, my office windows face a fire station. Sirens blared as Callie tried to talk with me. It took me a few minutes to piece together what she wanted.

She pointed at the Via Bearista Bear on the shelf near the window. She had three or four dollar bills in her hand, and she said she liked the Bearista Bear. "I've never seen one like that before."

I knew that she collected Starbucks Bearista Bears. My boss had mentioned this to me in passing some time ago.

Callie was trying to buy the Via Ready Brew Bearista Bear from Japan off of me. She seemed to think that four dollars would be a fair trade for the little Bearista Bear. Maybe in a normal world it would be. It was tragic in every way. I had to say no. I wasn't going to give up the little bear that Minori had given me. Minori had passed away less than a year ago. I still missed him.

She walked away from my office, dejected.

Chapter Twenty-Six: It's Crazy Good

Sometimes people email me tips about products they've seen in stores. Starbucks tests lots of new beverage, food, and sundry items all the time. There are small tests everywhere: Sweet Tea, Honey Vanilla Vivanno, Iced Cranberry Mocha. Before a beverage makes it to a national launch, it's usually gone through some kind of testing, somewhere.

I got a tip via Facebook that Starbucks now had their own Starbucks brand of root beer. This seemed a little strange to me. Starbucks root beer? Sodas handcrafted by baristas? The tipster gave me an address in Everett, Washington where I could find the root beer.

There was one problem. I had no way to get to Everett. My car wasn't running. My trusty 1993 Acura, which on a whim, had once taken me to Sacramento for the Honey Vanilla Vivanno, now needed a new timing belt. Rather than do the expensive repairs, my car sat parked in Jack's garage. Even worse, the last time I saw my car, I discovered the battery was dead too.

I had stopped driving[35]. In 2010, I moved into the retail core of downtown Seattle, which meant that Seattle Municipal Court and my office were now within a short walk of my apartment. It's even shorter if I take the bus tunnels. Urban living has some advantages. I can walk to Pike Place Market, to a million Starbucks stores, Pacific Place Mall, Westlake

---

35   I rationalized that since I spent no money on car insurance or gasoline, I had a little more money to spend at Starbucks each month.

Center, and an Evolution Fresh store too.

It was a Saturday afternoon, and I debated the various ways to get from Seattle to an Everett Starbucks to try "Starbucks Root Beer." Curiosity was killing me. There wasn't a bus that would take me directly to that store. Jack wouldn't be off work any time soon.

I dropped by the Pacific Place Starbucks on Sixth Avenue, ordered a Vanilla Latte, and sat down, debating the possibilities of who might like a trip up to Everett to try Root Beer. It was the kind of thing that not everyone was up for.

As I paid for my coffee, I mentioned to the register barista, Autumn, that what I really wanted was some Starbucks root beer.

She looked at me, puzzled.

"I hear that Starbucks is testing Root Beer in Everett. I really want to try it but my car is out of commission." Jack had volunteered to take me in the early evening hours, but I had hoped to get up to the store before it closed and I wasn't sure we'd make it in time.

"Let's go! I'll take you!" Autumn said.

I was stunned. I didn't know her at all. We'd only just met. She was a very new partner back then. Autumn had only been at Starbucks for a few months.

Still though, I wanted to go. She wanted to go. Why not? I wrote my cell phone number on a cup sleeve with a black Sharpie and said that I was totally game for a trip to Everett.

"I hope you can tolerate my car," Autumn warned.

"Of course I can. *You* have a car, and this is really nice of you to offer to go to Everett with me." I didn't tell her about the fact that my own car needed a timing belt, had a dead battery, and a fried electrical system.

"Great! I really want to try this Root Beer too! Starbucks Root Beer sounds very weird! I get off work in two hours, and I will text you then."

As promised, I got a text from Autumn, and we made arrangements to meet at my apartment, not far from Pacific Place. She swung by and I hoped in. I had no idea why she was so concerned about her car. At least her windows all rolled down.

The fried electrical in my car meant that I hadn't rolled my windows down in a number of years. It appeared that the worst problem with her old car was simply a malfunctioning turn signal. She apparently doesn't signal her lane changes. Ever.

Without a single hitch, we found our way to the store from the hot tip. Sure enough, I immediately saw signs for Starbucks Root Beer, Starbucks Ginger Ale, Sparkling Iced Teas, and Starbucks Lemon Ale.

Starbucks root beer is a really unique idea, I thought. I promptly took a few pictures of the exterior sandwich board, which was strategically placed to catch the eye of drive-thru customers.

We entered the store and ordered carbonated beverages. I tried the root beer. It was delicious: sugary sweet, bubbly, and wonderful. It was advertised as a spiced root beer, but I thought it was more sugary than spice. I'm not a fan of ginger ale, but Autumn - my new best friend at Starbucks – ordered one and we traded sips. Autumn enjoyed her Ginger Ale so much that she went back and ordered another carbonated drink.

Refreshers™ are light fruit juices with a green coffee extract mixed in. This adds a small amount of caffeine and gives the drink an iced tea feel. They come in flavors like Cool Lime and Valencia Orange. Autumn ordered a lemonade Refresher and asked the barista to carbonate it for her. It was amazing: sweet, cold, refreshing, and delicious.

We laughed and talked about all the things at Starbucks that could possibly be thrown into a carbonator, and I snapped some more photos of beverages. I imagined that carbonated iced coffee could be fun too.

"Hey, you can't take pictures in here!" yelled a voice, interrupting our good fun.

The woman in the green apron seemed kind of angry at us. I almost wanted to laugh. I had taken all the photos that I needed, so I stopped taking pictures.

I offered my two cents on the Starbucks photo policy. "You know you can take pictures in a Starbucks. There was a time many years ago-before Twitter, before official Starbucks Instagram and Pinterest profiles-that photos were a strict no-no at Starbucks, but that era has gone by. Starbucks is much more lenient now, coming to terms with the fact that everyone has a camera on their phone."

She didn't believe me. I'd obviously struck a chord. I had heard second-hand stories about partners being furious that I was photographing their store–not them–just the store. Look at this beautiful community table! Look at this gorgeous wall art! Most never said anything directly to me. On the other hand, I'd also heard gossip and second-hand tales of managers and district managers who loved seeing their stores featured on my blog. They had a lot of pride in their stores and liked seeing their hard work on my site. I understood that it could be unnerving for some partners who might not understand what I was trying to do.

My feeling was that if you really didn't want anyone to know about Starbucks Root Beer and carbonation, you wouldn't position a huge sandwich board sign on a public sidewalk near a drive through. That's an advertisement. Not a secret.

I assured her that I wouldn't take any more photos. The reality is that once something makes it outside of the R & D department at Starbucks Support Center and inside the stores, it's not a secret. And Starbucks was remarkably good at changing policies and adapting with the times. Starbucks is nimble.

I was a little too high on Starbucks Root Beer to let her angry voice bring down my fabulous bonding-over-root-beer-excursion with Autumn.

From my many conversations with Mallory in PR, the gist of the Starbucks photo policy, as I understood it, was this: *Don't take photos of anywhere in the store that isn't open to the public.* In other words, you shouldn't take photos of the back room, or of the refrigerator, or anything that a customer would not normally see. For this reason, I had avoided taking any photos of the actual Fizzio™ branded carbonation machine that I saw at a distance on a far counter behind the bar. You want to show off a beautiful community table, by all means, do so. *Don't video in the store*, was another media policy rule.[36].

We left. Autumn and I chatted more about life and Starbucks on the forty minute drive back to Seattle. I learned that Autumn was originally from Coeur D'Alene, Idaho, and came to Seattle looking for a bigger city experience.

Once I was home, I immediately wrote a blog article for StarbucksMelody.com.

I called the new Starbucks Root Beer "Crazy good."

I wish I had chosen my words more carefully. I didn't realize that I'd be quoted in the news calling the root beer "Crazy good." It sounded so silly. I became painfully aware that major media and possibly Starbucks investor analysts were all reading StarbucksMelody.com. I was very confused–were these people reading it all the time? Was this a one-time fluke? I wasn't sure.

---

36   Starbucks is nimble and quick to change policies and how things are done. Ask any partner, and they'll tell you that Starbucks changes things around all the time. The above is my understanding of the photo policy. It could change again.

A surprising news article appeared in BusinessWeek.com.[37]

An analyst based his "buy" rating of Starbucks stock on this tiny test of soda.

NEW YORK (AP) — A Janney Capital Markets analyst on Tuesday backed his "Buy" rating for Starbucks Corp., citing the company's test of a new soda product in a few locations and expectations for ongoing sales growth.

THE OPINION: Mark Kalinowski pointed to a post on the StarbucksMelody.com blog that the company is testing out "handcrafted" spiced root beer, lemon ale and ginger ale sodas at some of its stores, while also introducing carbonated versions of some of its existing beverages like iced tea.

I was shocked. Suddenly I was seeing several news articles[38][39] citing StarbucksMelody.com calling the new root beer "crazy good."[40]

A year after that adventure to Everett, Washington, the "Starbucks Carbonation" test has grown to more cities, and more markets, and has proven to be doing very well.

I'm still waiting patiently for Starbucks Fizzio™ carbonated drinks to make their way to Starbucks stores in Seattle. Ironically, it sometimes feels like we're the last city to get the latest Starbucks innovation.

---

37   http://www.businessweek.com/ap/2013-04-16/analyst-encouraged-by-starbucks-test-of-sodas

38   http://www.cnbc.com/id/100972133

39   http://www.fool.com/investing/general/2013/04/17/starbucks-wants-to-be-a-pop-star.aspx

40   http://www.businessinsider.com/starbucks-is-testing-fountain-drinks-2013-7

The Starbucks Root Beer adventure taught me a lot. I got to make friends with Autumn, who is now a shift supervisor in downtown Seattle. I was reminded that small things can create larger wakes than expected. In this case, without a doubt, I can say that I had no idea that the news would pick up on the Root Beer story so aggressively.

More generally, I'm reminded that in this day and age of social media and blogs, brick-and-mortar retailers never know when a customer is going to walk into their stores and trigger a little mainstream news surrounding their visit. Maybe that was extremely rare before Twitter, Facebook, blogs, and other social media sites, but in this day and age, it can happen unexpectedly, at any time, in many ways.

Be on the look at for Starbucks Root Beer in the future!

Bubble over with your experiences.

Chapter Twenty-Seven: All Great Things Start with a Seedling

In mid April 2013, I received an out-of-the-blue email from a Starbucks store partner in eastern Washington. These out-of-the-blue emails arrive more often than you might think. The partner told me she was organizing a community service project in Cle Elum, Washington. If you don't know Cle Elum, imagine the setting of *Northern Exposure*, the 1990s hit television series. A lot of it was filmed in Roslyn, which is near Cle Elum. Both Roslyn and Cle Elum are small towns with an abundance of fresh air, tall old-growth trees, and beautiful forest scenes all around.

In her email, the partner described the event: planting trees in areas that had been deforested by fire outside of Cle Elum. She said she really needed a lot more hands than had signed up. The event would take place in two weeks, on April 27, 2013, and she hoped I would help. I immediately replied in the affirmative. April 27 was a Saturday so I'd be off work. Cle Elum is a bit of a haul, but I would happily drive out there to help[41]. She invited me to stay at her house that Friday night and meet her dog "Starbuck". In the morning, we could carpool to the tree planting event. I was game, and I promised to spread the word.

On April 15, I posted a short blog article on StarbucksMelody.com to help promote what was now dubbed "Operation Lorax." My blog post

---

41   I still didn't have a working car yet, so I rented a car for the drive to Eastern Washington.

started with this snippet:

I am putting a call out for volunteers! Hopefully there are readers in Eastern Washington (or even Western Washington) who can help with this Starbucks-facilitated community service project in Cle Elum. I will be there! I signed up. So if you come out to re-plant trees, you'll see me there pitching in with a shovel, and working up a sweat.

A few days later, I received another email from the store partner. Guess what? She had persuaded Cliff to sign up for Operation Lorax! And now people were coming out of the woodwork to help. If you're Cliff Burrows, you have that magnetic pull.

With Starbucks, every event starts with coffee. There's a coffee tasting to kick off a new store, a publicity event, a new partner–anything and everything. It's a true Starbucks ritual.

I had no problem finding my way to Alexa's house, the eastern Washington partner who had invited me. I met her husband, her dog Starbuck, and spent the night in a cozy guest bedroom. And her kitchen was full of Starbucks coffee.

That Saturday, Alexa and I got up early for the event launch at an Ellensburg Starbucks. This small store off of Interstate 90 was full of hustle and bustle, with many partners on the floor, all anticipating their visit from Cliff Burrows.

Cliff arrived on time for the scheduled coffee tasting. I said hello to him, but he was busy talking to store partners, and it looked like a bad time to interrupt him. I said very little to him inside the store. Instead, I joined in the ceremonial coffee tasting.

A young Starbucks partner poured Tribute Blend from a French press into a million little sample cups. I thought it must be hugely nerve-wracking to be a young barista leading a coffee tasting with the President of

Just About Everything Starbucks right there as your guest of honor. Everything looked great, though, and she did a fine job of talking about the coffee and walking us through the familiar four steps of a coffee tasting.

Smell the Coffee.

Slurp the coffee, aerating it all over your mouth.

Locate where in your mouth you are tasting it.

Describe it.

While the barista pulled off a flawless performance, I remembered a story I'd heard about how Cliff and Howard can scare the living daylights out of young, newer partners. The story came from the 15th Avenue Coffee and Tea Starbucks Partner who had scolded me, "Never call him Howie!" That barista always had stories to tell.

The 15th Avenue Partner was covering a shift at the Madison Park location. She saw a young partner just leaving his shift, having worked a full day at the store. The young man had gone into the back of the store, removed his green apron, slung it over his arm, donned his jacket for the weather, and headed out the front door. He didn't quite make it. As he passed by the merchandise wall, he noticed that it wasn't neat and tidy and he stopped. Off the clock, without his apron and wearing his heavy jacket, he straightened up the merchandise.

At that moment, Cliff Burrows walked in. He saw the Starbucks partner–seemingly working–and barked out, "Hey partner, are you sporting a new dress code at work?" The young partner seemed shaken up.

He stammered, trying to explain that he wasn't going to leave his store a mess.

For what it's worth, I didn't think all that much of the story. I am sure it was a jarring moment for the young man straightening the merchandise wall. But I heard the story second-hand, and the lawyer in me is naturally very suspicious of hearsay. Moreover, I think every Fortune 500 corporation has stories of Big Executive walking in on Young Newbie Employee and jarring them to no end. It goes with the territory. Big Executives always have shoes that create little tremors (or monstrous earthquakes) wherever they go.

That's life. We hear stories and make assumptions about people before even meeting them. It doesn't mean that stories aren't retold without error. I recall a time, long before I met Cliff Burrows in real life, when I was suspicious of him. I'd been surprised that Starbucks brought in a person from a foreign Starbucks market (the UK) to manage such a huge and important job in the United States. Looking back, I see that was totally silly of me. I made a lot of incorrect assumptions about Starbucks before I began my blog. Writing StarbucksMelody.com forced me to learn about the brand. As I learned more, I understood why some of my earliest assumptions about Starbucks weren't always correct. I admire Cliff's integrity. That he would participate in a local tree planting project only reaffirmed my admiration. As I've said before and will say again, Cliff is a hero to me.

My coffee tasting musings ended as I came back to the reason for the gathering. We had trees to plant. Over 3,000 small seedlings awaited us. I hopped in a car with a store partner and joined a trail of cars headed to Cle Elum. To reach the area needing tree planting, we drove down a narrow, winding road, with a cliff on one side and a steep drop on the other. Fortunately, many people braved the drive: members of the greater-Ellensburg community, Red Cross volunteers, Starbucks volunteers, and ordinary customers like me.

It was a beautiful day, and lots of people wanted to take group photos. Someone took a photo of a small group from the Ellensburg Starbucks, including Cliff and me. I didn't know who took it, and I never saw the photo. Pictures and Starbucks events seemed to go hand in hand. I mumbled under my breath, "I hate having my picture taken."

Cliff overheard me and I heard him whisper, "Me, too." I knew that from experience.

At a Friends and Family Party for the then-new Brewery Blocks Starbucks in the heart of downtown Portland, Oregon, I caught Cliff at a rare moment when he wasn't busy with party-goers. I said, "Hey, let me take your pic for fun!" Always gracious, Cliff agreed. Trying to get a fun picture, I might have gone a little overboard. "Hey, stand against this wall. This would be a good backdrop!"

"Now smile, Cliff!"

"One more time!"

I realized I was testing his patience a bit. We took one more – a nice photo of him standing at the Brewery Blocks sign smiling for me, welcoming a brand new, gorgeous Starbucks store.

"Hey, you're not smiling much," I said to him later that night.

He laughed at me. He was in very good spirits, but acknowledged that he hated having his picture taken. I know that feeling only too well. I thanked him for his time, and he went on to mingle with others where he was subjected to more cameras. Being the President of Just About Everything Starbucks at a big event for a new store is pretty great, but there is a downside.

Having bonded over our mutual dislike of being photographed, I took the opportunity to chat with Cliff a bit more. Much later, a barista in a green apron explained to me exactly why Cliff doesn't like having his photo taken. Having no other explanation, I took her at her word. To get a picture you have to stand still a moment.

"Cliff doesn't like to stand still! Everybody knows this. If you want to talk with him, it's going to be let's walk and talk." That barista made a whirling motion with her hand and arm, like an engine that never slows down.

As we stood still waiting for tree planting to get going, I made small talk. "Cliff, when I stream investor conferences on the Investor Relations page at Starbucks.com[42], the analysts never ask the questions that I want to get answered." I was teasing him a bit. He knew it. There had been an investor conference a week earlier.

"What was it that you wanted to know, Melody?"

"When is Starbucks root beer going to be available at every single store? And I'd like to see more stores with the manual espresso Nuova Simonelli[43] machines."

This was my own personal wish list. Starbucks operates a handful of stores that use a special manual espresso machine made by a company called Nuova Simonelli.

Cliff chuckled. It isn't the kind of question that has an easy answer. "We have to see how the root beer does in testing."

I knew I would get that answer. Starbucks root beer was a small test beverage. I fully supported the idea of carbonation at Starbucks. Numerous combinations of the teas, juices, syrups, and more might lend themselves to a little fizziness.

As we watched some Red Cross volunteers organize backpacks of tiny tree seedlings, Cliff continued talking.

"You know that day was quite a day – the day of the conference with the New York analysts on the conference call. That morning I had gone to the Olympic Sculpture Park for more volunteering for the Global

---

42   http://investor.starbucks.com/phoenix.zhtml?c=99518&p=irol-irhome

43   http://nuovasimonelliusa.com/ - A Seattle business producing high quality espresso machines.

Month of Service."

I asked the natural follow up question, "What happened?" It was like a good, open-ended direct examination of a witness in a courtroom. When in doubt, always ask the question, "And then what happened?"

"I had been weeding that morning at the Olympic Sculpture Park in Belltown." This is a local Seattle park known for its art installations.

"You should have seen it. The weeds were growing this high." He motioned with his thumb and index finger, showing that the weeds must have been about two inches high. "And then I had to rush back to the SSC for the analysts call. I nearly didn't make it."

I had this image of Cliff pulling tenacious weeds at a Seattle park, and then, still in muddy jeans, fielding questions during a phone conference from significant Starbucks investors.

Returning my attention to Cle Elum, I noticed more pictures being taken as others set up a Starbucks tent. Every Starbucks community service event includes a tent with water and coffee available. Cliff jumped right in to help set up the tent. Mentally apologizing, I snapped a photo of him at work.

Pretty soon it was time to listen to instructions: how to locate special volunteers with backpacks of seedlings and how to dig in the dirt to plant the seedlings. As I wandered around with my shovel and seedlings, I met another customer who told me that he was a Subway store manager in Ellensburg. He had come out to volunteer because it was the right thing to do. Tree planting is easiest if you work in a team of two, so next thing I knew I was marching across a huge field, working up a sweat, and planting a lot of trees with the Subway store manager. We took turns with one of us shoveling and the other planting. Alexa, the partner who organized the event, stayed back near the main operations area, making sure that everything went smoothly without a hitch.

At a distance across the field, I saw Cliff with a shovel, right there with everyone else, planting tree seedlings.

After we collectively planted over 3,000 tree seedlings, a group of Ellensburg fire fighters came out to greet us and thank us for our work. These were the firefighters who had fought the wildfires that had deforested this area of eastern Washington. It was a very moving moment. Then we cleaned up, put shovels back in cars, took another round of photos (this time a huge group photo of every Operation Lorax volunteer), and dispersed – tired, but very satisfied.

The very next day, I posted a blog article on StarbucksMelody.com, complete with lots of photos. It started as follows:

Starbucks partners (and many others) planted 3,050 trees as part of a re-forestation project during the Starbucks Global Month of Service. Less than one year ago, the Taylor Bridge Fire did a great deal of damage to the Cle Elum area of Eastern Washington. I would say that over 100 Starbucks partners, a number of customers, and other volunteers worked to plant trees in a damaged field.

I have to give a ton of credit to the Starbucks store manager who brought many people together...

As I sit at my desk writing these words, over a year has passed since Operation Lorax. I still look back on it fondly. That blog post is one of my favorites. I haven't had a reason to return to Cle Elum, but I've heard from Starbucks partners that the trees are doing well.

All great things start with a seedling.

Chapter Twenty-Eight: When Frenchmen Talk of Croissants

In May of 2013, I got another invitation to the Starbucks headquarters. Once again, Mallory emailed me. Emails from her set off a Pavlovian reaction.

"We'd like for you to come try our new French recipe baked goodies."

At the very end of 2012, Starbucks spent a lot of money to buy a San Francisco bakery called La Boulange. The plan was to overhaul the food offerings, make them with fewer and more natural ingredients, and make them taste better. Eventually, every Starbucks would offer bakery items developed by Pascal Rigo, the founder of the La Boulange bakery.

The introduction of La Boulange into stores was slow and judicious. Seattle got their La Boulange items before many other areas of the country. Before the big kick off of La Boulange foods in Seattle, Mallory and the Starbucks PR people invited me and a bunch of bloggers and media people to an event to try all the new foods at the headquarters. Pascal Rigo would speak to us personally.

I joined up with a group on the 9th floor. By now, I'd been here a million times and I was used to it. Coming to the headquarters was old hat. Too bad, unlike Disneyland Parks, you can't buy an annual pass to the Starbucks headquarters. There were indeed E-Ticket rides here. The Cupping Room. The Alcoves of Store Products. The Coffee Gear Store. The Starbucks inside a Starbucks. The Coffee Roaster. The Tea Tasting

Room. There were secret laboratory and innovation rooms too. Granted, it's not quite the Haunted House, the Matterhorn, Space Mountain, and It's A Small World, but it's close enough for me.

I was escorted to a large dining room table, set with plates and French presses of Starbucks Organic Yukon Blend, a core Starbucks coffee. I only knew one of the other bloggers and media people at the table: Beautiful Existence. That really is her name. She was a blogger on a one year challenge to eat all Starbucks food. I'd met her before. Her goal was to spend all of 2013 eating Starbucks food and *only* Starbucks food. I couldn't quite imagine it. I'd miss the chance to grab a cup of Tom Douglas' famous tomato soup at the Dahlia Bakery in Seattle, Beecher's mac and cheese, and Fran's Chocolates. Her definition of Starbucks food included every brand that Starbucks operated. She counted Evolution Fresh, Teavana, Tazo, La Boulange, Seattle's Best Coffee, Starbucks Evenings food, and Roy Street all as Starbucks Food.

Don't misunderstand. Her diet wasn't limited to turkey-bacon breakfast sandwiches, coffee, pastries, and tea. Her diet could include lovely spinach salads from Evolution Fresh juice bars, chicken flatbreads and mac and cheese from the Starbucks Evenings stores, and of course beer and wine. Even so, it's still a very limited diet for a whole year. You'd never get to enjoy a fish taco, for example, and Seattle has amazing local fish. But it wasn't a life limited to lattes and breakfast sandwiches either.

One-year challenges have been a pretty trendy thing to do in the world of blogging. I wondered if I'd made a mistake in my own blog. I had no theme. I walked into store. Took photos of pretty stores. Wrote blog posts. Wrote about drinks and test beverages. Wrote about coffee seminars. Lather. Rinse. Repeat. I had no thematic destination, unlike Beautiful's blog, *For One Year of My Life*[44]. My attitude is live and let live. She

---

44   http://for1yearofmylife.com/

seemed to genuinely enjoy her one year Starbucks eating challenge.

Pascal Rigo sat down right next to me, at the head of the table. There he was. The French baker. Dark beautiful hair, cute French accent. . . you can only imagine. He was gorgeous. And here he was next to me talking about butter, sugar, and flour. Never before had butter sounded so sexy to me. While I'd been intoxicated by the Siren before, this was the first time my heart went *pitter patter*.

Several corporate Starbucks partners, including Mallory, offered us tray after tray of food, so we'd get the chance to try the best of everything that La Boulange had to offer. The only thing that prevented me from grossly overeating was that I was attempting to take photos of everything before the food entered my mouth. That, and the distraction of the French man next to me who took his chocolate croissants pretty darn seriously.

After we'd sampled all the new French recipe items, we socialized as a group for a bit. Beautiful Existence commented that the small tomato cheese croissants were like a mini pizza croissant. I looked forward to the idea of being able to buy some savory croissants at Starbucks. I thought she was a brave person for living her life inside these challenges. She told me that she had them all mapped out. Imagine all the big corporations that she'd be surprising. "Surprise! I'm going to be immersed in your corporation for one year and get a lot of publicity doing so."

I wondered if there was some option to live a Disneyland life for one year. Perhaps because I was raised close to Anaheim, California, I dreamt a little too much of Mickey Mouse, Main Street Disney, and Tomorrow Land.

As it turned out, after finishing a one-year challenge of eating all Starbucks food, (and getting an enormous amount of publicity for it), Beautiful Existence went on to start her year of learning all the sports that one can learn at REI. She'll be extremely physically fit after the 2014 REI one-year challenge. Beautiful Existence mentioned to me that she had a decade's worth of one year challenges planned.

I was jarred out of my contemplation of possible one-year challenges to find that it was photo-op time with the handsome Frenchman Pascal Rigo. I think it had been Beautiful's idea. She handed her camera to a Starbucks corporate person, and asked for her photo with the handsome Frenchman. I decided I might as well too, and so photo-op time continued as I watched numerous Starbucks partners putting away left over croissants, mini loaves, and cookies.

I wondered what else Pascal might do with all that wonderful butter?

As soon as I left the headquarters, I called up Jack. I felt compelled to tell him of the handsome Frenchman who talked of croissants. I knew he'd get a good laugh. It was the middle of the day, so I knew exactly where he'd be: three hundred feet high in his tower crane. He's a tower crane operator. He can't easily go anywhere. He tells me stories of getting out of the cab and walking the boom to decorate it with Christmas lights. We've had these conversations enough that I know he's tied off with a harness and safety line that runs the length of the boom, but it still sounds so dangerous to me. If I call him when he's in his three-hundred foot office in the sky, our conversations are often broken up by a voice I hear in the background. "Bring it up easy to the left Jack."

Many times I've told him that he shouldn't answer his phone when he's swinging tons of steel in the air. The breaks in the day as a load gets loaded or unloaded from the boom, and the magic of Bluetooth allows him to answer anyway. Sometimes I catch him on his coffee break. As you might have guessed, he carries a large thermos of Starbucks coffee up there high with him. French Roast or Sumatra gets him through the day.

Sure enough, he got a good laugh at the afternoon's events.

Jack's order at Starbucks has not changed in twenty years: Double Short Breve Latte. I have never seen him order a Frappuccino. He's never used a Starbucks card. And no matter how wonderful the croissants are, he's probably not going to buy the food. Just give him a lovely Double Short Breve Latte, and all is well.

As much as things change, they stay the same too.

Chapter Twenty-Nine: Happy Birthday Howard Schultz

For the past several years, I've been sending Howard Schultz a "Happy Birthday" email on July 19. According to Wikipedia, that's his birthday. I hope Wikipedia is correct. I would probably send Cliff Burrows a birthday email each year too if I had any idea when his birthday was. Perhaps I should ask.

I deduced Howard's email address eons ago. It wasn't hard. Once I knew the pattern of initials and last name at Starbucks.com, Howard's email address became obvious to me. So Howard receives an annual "Happy Birthday" email from me.

On the morning of July 19, 2013, I started an email to Howard, then scrapped it. I wondered why I should even bother. Howard probably receives thousands of birthday emails – there are over three thousand staff partners at corporate headquarters, not to mention all the Starbucks offices and stores around the country and around the world. My email probably gets buried in a staggering avalanche of emails. He probably wouldn't even notice my email, let alone send me a reply.

So off I went to work. It was just another day for me, with hearings in the morning in court and desk work in the afternoon. After a productive day I returned home for a quiet evening. I planned to join a friend on a couple-hour boat cruise of Portage Bay and Lake Union the next morning. I never tire of seeing the houseboat featured in the movie *Sleepless in Seattle.* I'm a hopeless romantic about Seattle.

When ten o'clock rolled around, I realized that I still hadn't sent Howard Schultz his birthday email. With only two hours left in Howard's birthday. If didn't send it soon it wasn't going to happen. *Screw you, Howard Schultz,* I thought. *It's not like you send me a birthday email or write on my Facebook page every May 17. You're not getting an email from me, Howard!* Mid-stream, I realized how silly I was being. Howard has 200,000 employees and millions of fans. I would send the email, just to keep up my annual tradition.

And so I caved. I only wrote like two sentences, but the email did wish him a happy birthday. I stewed a little longer, but shortly before hitting the sack, I clicked *send* on my annual *Happy Birthday, Howard Schultz email.* I slept like a rock. When I awoke the next morning, I made a cup of coffee with my Verismo coffee maker, a single-serve machine produced by Starbucks. Eventually, I sat down at my computer, checking my email. As a matter of routine, I faithfully view my email every morning.

Lo and behold, there was an email waiting for me from Howard Schultz.

Damn you, Howard Schultz. You proved me wrong once again.

I opened his email. Howard thanked me for my email. It was a very simple thank you, signed "Best, Howard."

I was glad I hadn't given up my annual tradition.

Life's too short to drink bad coffee or forget birthdays.

Chapter Thirty: Do You Know About This Coffee?

On a hot August Saturday, I set off on a walk from my apartment to Roy Street Coffee and Tea, which is operated by Starbucks. This wasn't merely a casual jaunt, this was a quest.

Earlier in the week, I'd received Facebook messages and seen status updates about a special whole bean coffee. A Facebook message had enthusiastically told me that I had to try Starbucks Reserve coffee Micro Blend 11. As I understood it, only two locations were offering this coffee: one in New York City, and the other in Seattle's Capitol Hill neighborhood, Roy Street Coffee and Tea.

The story I heard was this: Starbucks roasted Micro Blend 11 for the business area that delivers freshly roasted coffee to fine restaurants. Starbucks roasted a little more than what the restaurant needed and so the left over Micro Blend 11 went to the two Starbucks stores.

Roy Street opened in November 2009. It operates as a Starbucks learning laboratory. It's one of the places I always mention when I'm asked, "What Starbucks sights should I visit when I come to Seattle?" Inside, you'll find Starbucks coffees, but the atmosphere is nothing like Starbucks. The food menu doesn't resemble Starbucks. All the food comes from a local Seattle business called The Essential Bakery – you won't find a sausage breakfast sandwich anywhere in Roy Street. The espresso machine is a manual Nuova Simonelli, made by a Seattle company specializing in high-end industrial use manual espresso machines. The baristas have no apparent dress code. There are no green aprons. You can pay with any Starbucks Card and earn a star for each transaction, but that's where the similarity with Starbucks ends.

Lucky for me, the Roy Street store manager, Evan, was working. When I asked about this special coffee, he went in the back and brought out two bags of the very scarce, and heavily revered, Micro Blend 11. "These are my last two bags, Melody." He went on to explain that it was a blend of Sun Dried Ethiopia, the finest in the country, with the best Guatemala coffee. I purchased the last two bags of coffee and ordered a cup (they had an open bag for single cup orders) to go with my breakfast of an egg Stromboli sandwich. The coffee lived up to its reputation. It was jammy in the mouth, and full of Bing cherry and cocoa notes. All the lovely flavors of these beans were born of the magic of the growing regions, the magnificent processing, and roasting. Happily sipping and eating, I was able to catch up with Evan, whom I hadn't seen in a while. Sadly, I don't drop by as often as I would like. I remind myself to visit more, but the problem is that there is only one of me and many stores that I want to visit all the time.

From Roy Street, I walked a short distance to the newest Starbucks in Seattle – the one at the corner of Pike and Broadway. I knew that store manager, too, and hoped to run into him. Carrying my small plain paper bag containing the last two bags of prestigious Micro Blend 11 coffee, I went into Pike and Broadway, looking for the store manager. I decided to hang out for a few minutes. I ordered a Cool Lime Refresher and played Words With Friends on my phone.

In walked Howard Schultz. I was preoccupied by a close game on my phone, but Howard's tall figure drew my attention. I overheard him making small talk with the register barista, who sounded a bit nervous.

She was trying to explain to him that the molding along the ceilings was original, preserved, and restored for this store's very old building location. He was patient and listened attentively, though I thought it was likely he was already aware of the design features of this store – and probably every Seattle Starbucks.

When he finished the conversation with the barista, Howard noticed me and dropped by my seat to say hello. He asked me what I thought of the store, and I said it was beautiful. At that moment, I exclaimed, "Hey Howard, look at this coffee I got." I pulled a bag of the Micro Blend 11 out of my brown paper sack. "I bought the last of it at Roy Street."

Howard Schultz's eyes sparkled. "Melody, you'll love this coffee." His face was filled with genuine coffee passion. "It's extraordinary." Howard paused, leaning into me, and asked, "Do you know about this coffee?"

"No, I don't." I managed to say that with a straight face, despite the fact that I had just heard all about it from the store manager at Roy Street Coffee. I've decided that when Howard Schultz asks you if you want to hear about something, you don't cut him off. He could have said to me, "Melody, do you know about this thing called gravity that keeps us from flying off the earth?" and my answer would have been the same, "No, I don't Howard. Tell me about it."

Deep inside, a part of me was sad that Minori never got a moment like this.

Connect. Discover. Respond.

Chapter Thirty-One: An Evening with Sheryl Crow

On September 17, 2013, I received this email from My Starbucks Rewards.

I had to stare at it for a long time to be sure it was real. Was it a scam? It almost didn't look real to me. A private Sheryl Crow concert for me and the best MyStarbucksRewards customers? I pinched myself.

I don't know how I ended up so lucky. The email said I could invite one person. Earlier that year, Sessily had relocated from Eureka, California to Silverdale, Washington. Silverdale is a bit of a haul from Seattle, but I thought she might want to go with me. It would be a great chance to catch up outside of Facebook status updates.

I sent Sessily a text message. The reply back was immediate. Yes, she wanted to see Sheryl Crow with me, despite that she was scheduled for an opening shift that morning. It was a little bit difficult to arrange the logistics because of the "surprise" location, but we agreed to meet up at my work that afternoon and then go together from there to the Sheryl Crow concert.

The location for the concert was going to come in at the last minute, so Sessily had some time in my office, admiring Starbucks artifacts everywhere. It hardly looked like an attorney's office. There were mugs of Starbucks yesteryear, a poster of a Pumpkin Spice Latte on my wall, and the Via Bearista Bear on a shelf.

The venue announcement came: Roy Street Coffee and Tea.

Roy Street was crowded, but the small subset of customers waving special concert invites in their hand could not have numbered more than thirty or forty. A large number of Starbucks corporate partners turned out for the event. No Cliff Burrows. I had hoped he would have the chance to meet Sessily. Perhaps someday he will make it over to Silverdale to meet her for a French press of some amazing Starbucks Reserve coffee.

I introduced Sessily to every SSC partner that I recognized. There were a few people from the coffee department. Arthur Rubinfeld, the executive in charge of all things Evolution Fresh and emerging brands, was there, along with a few people from the PR and marketing department. I think there might have been a one to one ratio of corporate partners to special invitee guests.

Sessily and I whispered back and forth to each other, treating the corporate partners as if they were celebrities. "I want to meet them all!" she said.

There was a moment when Arthur Rubinfeld looked unoccupied, so I took that chance to introduce Sessily to him. I didn't really introduce myself first. I pretty much assumed that he knew who I was, even though I'd only had a few interactions with Arthur over the years.

"Hey I want you to meet someone," I said, and explained that Sessily was an amazing partner who had transferred from California to Silverdale, Washington.

"Arthur, she made up her own custom blend of Starbucks coffees – it's the Pacific Coast Highway Blend."

"I would love to do a tasting for you of my blend," Sessily said excitedly. I hoped he would take her up on it. She's excellent at baking treats to go with coffees too.

The whole idea of custom blends from existing Starbucks coffees has become an increasingly uncommon conversation topic over the years. Often times, store partners don't consider the idea of re-blending their coffees. In fact, some mainstays of the Starbucks core coffee lineup came from re-blending existing coffees. To this day, customers everywhere love Caffè Verona coffee, which includes Italian Roast and Yukon Blend as its main components. Once upon a time, Starbucks sold a coffee called Viennese Blend, which was really a blend of House Blend and French Roast.

I knew from years of keeping up with Sessily that she was good at this art of re-blending existing coffees.

"Sure! I'd love a coffee tasting," Arthur said. In the back of my mind, I thought *that'll never happen.* He didn't offer her an email address to connect, and so the whole thing seemed like the kind of pleasantry that's supposed to happen at a party. My gut also told me that he was just too busy. By the same token, I didn't think that I'd ever have more than a stolen few minutes of Howard or Cliff's time: they're too busy.

Sessily and I had the chance to introduce ourselves to Sheryl Crow during a pre-arranged special meet and greet for the invited MyStarbucksRewards customers. It was time to get in that line, which looked like a receiving line, about ten people deep. Everybody got their turn.

Sessily and I brought up the rear of the line. Each person had the chance to have their photo taken with Sheryl Crow as well as a few minutes of conversation. During our chatting earlier in the day, I had confided in Sessily that this would be the second time I'd met Sheryl Crow.

"Really? When was the first time?"

"I can't even remember the year, it was so long ago, but it was the mid-1990s I think. I was working as a dental assistant. I was working with a periodontist who had relocated from L.A. to Seattle, and one day she said, 'Sheryl Crow is coming in to get her teeth cleaned.'"

"I don't think I even got the chance to say anything to Sheryl Crow, but I sat there assisting and admiring her perfect teeth and gums," I confessed. It was a funny story that made Sessily laugh. I told the story to Sheryl Crow herself during the meet and greet. Sheryl Crow had no idea who I was, but when I mentioned the name of the dentist whom she befriended in the 1990s, she laughed and told me that she remembered going to the dentist once in Seattle.

Sheryl Crow began the show with her big hit song from the 1990s, "All I Wanna Do." When she sang "Every Day is a Winding Road" and got to the lyrics *I've been living off of coffee and nicotine* she pointed at her

Starbucks paper cup. Turns out Sheryl Crow is genuinely a fan of Starbucks, though she commented that when she goes to Starbucks, her son doesn't like the new lemon loaf without icing on it. I guess La Boulange is not for Sheryl Crow's little boy.

Sheryl proudly let the audience know that she has a Gold Card and that her favorite beverage is a *Triple Venti Non-Fat Latte*.

It was pretty amazing to hear a performance by Sheryl Crow for a group of less than one hundred people – and the MyStarbucksRewards invitees were given priority seating in the front rows.

As if you could possibly be confused whether Starbucks was sponsoring this, the official Starbucks partners working the event brought a small My Starbucks Rewards sign with them!

All I can say is that this was a pretty amazing thing for Starbucks to do. Thank you Starbucks.

Reward your fans. Create magical moments.

Chapter Thirty-Two: This is the House that Jack Built

It was a typical cold, November day in Seattle. It wasn't raining, but it was heavy coat weather. This was another very ordinary weekend in the life of Melody. People think that I spend all my time at Starbucks, but it isn't really true.

My friend Rose and I were scheduled for lunch at a swanky new Japanese-inspired restaurant at Sixth and Lenora, on the edge of downtown Seattle. The restaurant is a Tom Douglas restaurant, though I didn't immediately recognize it as such because there's no obvious signage that tells you that. The whole block along Lenora has these super high luxury apartments – the kind where people easily spend over $2,000 a month in rent. The bottom floor had stores and this new restaurant.

I thought it was the coolest thing in the world. Part of the reason I loved it was that Jack's tower crane had been set up on this site for a long time. I wished I lived here. Then I'd be able to tell my visitors, "This is the house that Jack built."

There are a few buildings all over Seattle where I walk by and think, "Jack built that." Jack built the parking garage connected to the Target along Northgate Way in Seattle. Once I attempted to wave at him from 300 feet below, thinking I would catch his attention with my waving arms. I probably looked like a crazy person on the sidewalk. You can't get the attention of a crane operator a block away in the sky. It doesn't work.

And you can't live in a Target, but you can live in this high-rise apartment building. This is the house that Jack built. And the restaurant that Jack built.

The lobby has huge double doors that look like they need a doorman. Rose was early. I'm often a tad bit late. I rushed in to find her waiting for me.

"Hey Melody, guess who is here?" she asked me.

I had no idea. Seattle is like a big small town, despite having a population of 600,000 people. You can easily run into people in this city.

"Howard Schultz?" I guessed Howard because well, it *is* possible to run into him in this city, and he's someone we'd both easily recognize.

"No, no silly! Tom Douglas is here. I saw him. He's sitting at the bar – it looks like he's watching TV."

Rose turned and pointed behind her. I couldn't see him from where we stood.

I took a couple steps forward and then I saw him. You can't really miss Tom Douglas. He's as iconic to Seattle as any other local celebrity. If he had a white beard, he'd look like Santa Clause. Santa Tom would carry donuts, coconut cream pie, and small containers of tomato soup instead of presents in his red sack.

Together, Rose and I headed into the new Tanaka San restaurant. We walked right past Tom Douglas, who was still watching TV in the bar area of the restaurant. I'd eaten at many Tom Douglas restaurants before, but this was the first time I'd seen him at one. I followed Tom Douglas on Twitter, though I was sure that Tom had hired a social media person that tweets for him.

A twenty-something waitress seated the two of us, handing us paper menus. Paper menus are perfect for autographs. "Rose, I'm going to go ask Tom Douglas for his autograph!" I bolted upright and headed out of the restaurant back to the bar area. Tom was still there.

Rose followed behind me. This is something she'd never do without me. She gets nervous parking for more than five minutes in the loading zone in front of my apartment.

"Hi Tom!" I called out his name. He turned and looked at me. I was bubbling over, and told him that I was a big fan. I wished I prepared something more eloquent to say, but he got that gist that I enjoy eating at his restaurants. My smile stretched from ear to ear.

"Would you mind autographing my menu?"

He appeared to be flattered. It was clear he didn't know me from Adam. And why would he? While I'd seen him speak at the Starbucks Thanksgiving Blend event many years ago, I'd never met him before.

In a flash, he had a Sharpie in his hand. You have that power when you're Tom Douglas. You ask for things and people bring them to you.

Rose, who was immediately behind me, asked the same of him. He was incredibly gracious and autographed both of our menus. When we sat back down at our table, I tweeted a picture of my autographed menu to the official Tom Douglas Twitter profile[45].

Rose ordered a special cold-brewed coffee that was on the menu. The waitress explained that it was a blend of Willow Blend and House Blend Starbucks coffees, very slowly brewed over 24 hours, in a series of tubes and bottles, and dripped into a final container. We studied the device and it looked more like a mad scientist's invention than something used to brew coffee. The end product was delicious. I had some of Rose's cold-brewed coffee and kicked myself that I had not ordered the same.

I couldn't wait to return with Sessily. I knew she'd love the place. And probably would try to diagram the cold coffee brewer, so she could at-

---

45   https://twitter.com/TomDouglasCo

tempt a home version of the same thing.

And that is the story of the house (and restaurant) that Jack built.

Chapter Thirty-Three: Pine Street Christmas Card

It was the day after Christmas 2013. A normal work day for me. I was on my way home from work and decided to drop by the Pine Street Starbucks. The store manager, Debbie, was working.

"Melody, wait, we have something for you," she said. Moments later, she handed me a red envelope with my name on it. It was sealed, but had that distinctive Christmas card look.

Sure enough, it was a Christmas card, signed by most of the store's partners. There were lots of kind and sweet words written inside. I had to really linger with it. It's incredibly thoughtful for a store to give a customer a Christmas card. I felt like it should be the other way around. There was a Starbucks gift card inside of it. I didn't know the amount, but it didn't matter. I was totally touched by these store partners.

I took a photo of the card and uploaded it to my blog's Facebook page. I knew that if I did that, the store's district manager, who thoroughly reads my blog and Facebook page, would see it. I wanted her to know how thoughtful the store had been.

"A Christmas Season Made Bright By Joy And Love" read the front of the card, and inside were partners who thanked me for being a great customer.

The magic of Starbucks is in the stores. There are great connections being made. I realized at that moment that there were times when I'd lost sight of that vision. A few minutes of Howard's time seemed less important to me now. I could never give Minori what he didn't get. I never stopped being impressed with Howard and Cliff for the leaders that they are, but the magic doesn't come from leaders up high in the organization. The magic is in the day to day interactions in the stores and the things that Starbucks does to give their local communities. I was feeling pretty content.

On New Year's Day, I drove out to the Silverdale Starbucks to visit Sessily[46]. We had talked about tasting the new Casi Cielo coffee together, and she said she'd prepared a special food pairing. I met up with her in late morning. She dropped by my table and gave me a present – a special "Shared Moments" holiday Starbucks mug that was only sold in a few select retailers. It was very pretty. We both thought that some of Starbucks holiday items sold by other retailers, such as grocery stores, Target, and places like Bed Bath & Beyond, looked better than the merchandise in the brick-and-mortar Starbucks stores.

She made a French press of Casi Cielo. It was much roastier than I remembered from years past. Then we tried her homemade Macaroons with chocolate and lemon. They were so delicious. Sessily's Instagram feed constantly tempted me with her amazing baking skills – from cupcakes to cookies, she knew how to bake.

Today she was adorned with a gold plastic wing in her hair and her eye makeup sparkled. On some people, this might look gaudy, but on Sessily it worked perfectly. I adored her. I liked her kindness, her generosity, her enthusiasm for Starbucks, and her upbeat personality.

I loved connecting over the French press of Casi Cielo, even though we both remarked that this year's was quite different. "Can you believe

---

46   After a long time of not having a car, I had a new car by January 2014.

it's been almost four years since I took that drive to Eureka, California to meet you?" I asked. She promptly reminded me that my phone call to her store had interrupted her from cleaning floor drains.

I'd jump at the chance to sit down with Howard and share a French press of coffee. But my priorities remained with what happens inside the stores. What was important that I kept in touch with people like Sessily. She was only in the area while her husband was temporarily stationed at Bremerton Naval Station. I was lucky that over the years I had gotten to know her, she managed to move closer to me.

New Year's Day 2014. I had started it off right. Coffee and a friend. I crossed my fingers for more nice conversation, coffee pairings, and kind people like Sessily and the partners at Pine Street in my life.

The magic is in the stores.

Chapter Thirty-Four: January 3, 2014

I headed into work, as usual. As part of my unvarying routine, I stopped at a Starbucks on my way in. Today was a short Clover-brewed Ethiopia coffee and a bagel. I entered the bus tunnel connecting the Westlake Station to Pioneer Square, while juggling my heavy purse and coffee.

When I got off the bus, I saw a former client, Jacob Smith. I knew him well. He was dressed in ragged clothes with a scruffy gray beard and heavy, tired eyes. His jacket had rips and holes in the arms of it. He looked like the stereotype of an older, poor, mentally ill person.

I had represented him many times in Mental Health Court, where he had regular court reviews. Eventually his probation had to be struck because Western State Hospital psychologists had opined that he was too mentally ill to understand what was happening in a courtroom.

It was true. Conversations with him could be difficult to follow. Sometimes he made no sense. I had read the forensic reports and knew he had some fixed delusions. I knew he was harmless though.

I stopped and said hello to Jacob. A part of me loved him. I'd spent two years representing him off and on in those court reviews. I knew he was kind. He smiled at me, but seemed confused.

"Where do I know you from?" he asked.

I explained that I had been his attorney in court – and I reminded him of the names of some of the other attorneys on the mental health court team.

"It's confusing isn't it? You did have several different attorneys when you were in court," I reassured him.

Jacob remembered his previous probation officer and then remembered who I was.

"How are you, Jacob?"

"I got to the Mission last night. I got a chair. I slept. There were no more beds so I slept upright in a chair," he mumbled.

He meant Seattle's Union Gospel Mission, a well-used emergency shelter in Pioneer Square. I tried to ask him where he was going this morning, but his answer was unintelligible.

My heart broke. I set down my coffee and bagel on the bus tunnel bench, freeing up my hands to dig through my purse. I knew that I had a $10 Subway card buried in there somewhere. I had put it there precisely for these moments. I couldn't do everything, but I could always do something. I felt compelled to give. I gave him the Subway card, he thanked me, and then I gave him a big hug.

I had to hurry into work. I had started my day right. I knew it didn't matter if I ran into Jacob or Howard Schultz. It was all the same. Either way, I'd feel like that was a fine start to the day.

I plopped into my office chair, which sunk a bit on me. At some point in the past few weeks, my office chair had broken on me, and wouldn't stay up. It was a nuisance. I listened to the constant noise from Fourth Avenue South below me. I looked at the Via Ready Brew Bearista Bear on my shelf, collecting dust.

I picked it up and brushed it off. I found a little yellow post-it note, and wrote the words "Callie, enjoy your new Bearista Bear. Hope your 2014 is a beautiful new year." Then I took the post-it note and the bear, and stuffed them into her box in the mailroom.

You can always do something to make another person's day.

Chapter Thirty-Five: First Female President of the United States

It was January 2014. The Via Bearista Bear in my office was gone. I thought about my job, which I loved. I remembered back to one of the funnier episodes from my experiences in Seattle Municipal Court's Mental Health Court.

Frequently, people ask me, "Why don't you work for Starbucks?"

I usually shrug off the question with a quick reply. "I love my career as an attorney." For most people, that's enough to end the discussion. No matter what they think I do with my days, they are satisfied that I have a career and understand that Starbucks is not in the stars for me.

Some people push further. "But Starbucks has a legal department. Why in the world don't you go work there?" At that point, I try to explain that I have been practicing criminal defense law for many years and that I might be lost in the world of contract law and corporate law.

All that is true. But a fuller and more meaningful answer requires some explanation. The first part of the explanation can be summed up by the familiar expression *Ignorance is Bliss.* I suspect that working for Starbucks could kill the joy and fun of being a fan. Having grown up a short distance from Disneyland, I'm a fan of all-things Disney, but I have no interest in working there. It would be crushing to learn that my rosy image of Mickey Mouse is wrong. What if Mickey and Minnie smoke cigarettes, have short tempers, and curse like sailors?

Deep inside the Starbucks headquarters at 2401 Utah Avenue South, the Starbucks Siren could reveal failings that I don't want to know about. She could be cranky and impatient. *Let me just be a fan, please.*

The second part of the explanation is more difficult to capture in a sound bite. I work in a mental health court, which is a tiny micro-niche in the world of criminal defense. Once in a blue moon, I meet criminal defense attorneys who look at me with disdain, as if my job is an anathema to them. You have to *collaborate* with the prosecutor. There are no trials. "You're going nowhere if you work in a courtroom with no trials," I've been told by some extremely adversarial defense attorneys. It's as if they see no value in working together.

But I love my job, and I can see the difference I make in people's lives.

Seattle Municipal Court's Mental Health Court is a consolidated competency court. It was the fourth in the whole country, established in 1999. Even today, few mental health courts have a two-track program, evaluating trial competency, and encouraging treatment.

The competency track of the court is for clients who are so mentally ill that they lack the ability to work with an attorney and understand the court process. These people are often so delusional that they believe that micro-chips have been implanted in them or that they have super powers. This group of people are sometimes very paranoid and fearful of conspiracies. Rarely do they have any insight into their mental illness. I find these cases heart-breaking. Fortunately, only a tiny fraction of cases fall into this category.

The treatment program is for the vast majority of people who are higher functioning and have the ability to manage their mental illness, much like people with diabetes or asthma manage their chronic health conditions. These clients have exchanged their right to a jury trial for the opportunity to receive probation and treatment. Mental health court probation officers work with community treatment providers to ensure that clients stay engaged with any required treatment, keep appointments, and remain clean and sober. Clients return to court often for judge-monitored reviews. I see these types of clients all the time. Many are very nice working people who simply need support to manage their illnesses.

A mental health court that doesn't treat both the competency cases and treatment cases doesn't see all of the most mentally ill clients. One advantage of the two track mental health court system is that a judge can order an individual charged with a serious offense to be restored to a hospital, to reach a healthier mental state. If a client restores after hospitalization, he or she might then choose to maintain their mental health by working with our treatment program.

Seattle Mental Health Court really works. We can get people involved in much needed treatment. Using a small transitional housing program, we can sometimes get a homeless person a roof over his or her head. It's hard not to be saddened when a person says that he or she slept by a dumpster, in a doorway, or on concrete.

A few years ago, during the week of Christmas, it seemed like most Seattle Municipal Court judges were on vacation. Pro Tem judges were filling in everywhere. A Pro Tem judge is a like a substitute teacher in the world of courtrooms. They wear a black robe for a day when a judge is sick or on vacation.

Sitting in the courtroom, waiting for my cases to be called, I saw a familiar face emerge from the back-room holding area, the small locked rooms with a stainless steel toilet where the criminally accused wait for their turn in front of the judge.

I've represented her many times, I thought. This woman in jail garb and handcuffs was a frequent flyer. Her crimes consisted of thefts of food when hunger overtook her. I assumed that it was the same scenario today, though another attorney was representing her so I didn't know the underlying facts of the case.

The Pro Tem judge was not familiar with expert doctor's reports on mental illness–or the process of a colloquy to find the criminally-accused person "not competent." He asked the woman an open-ended question. "Do you have anything you want to tell the court?" he asked in a stern voice, as if this very mentally ill woman would suddenly grasp the severity of the situation.

Still handcuffed, the woman stood up and turned in a circle, giving the entire courtroom a very serious looking over. She placed her hand over her heart, as best she could with her wrists in cuffs. With great confidence, she said, "I'd like to thank the good people of the State of Washington for electing me the first female president of the United States."

Yes, I love Starbucks. But I cannot trade this for a free pound of coffee each week. I hope to stay where I am for a long time to come. I'll take an ONWARD t-shirt and pass on the job[47].

Pursue the job you love. Love the job you pursue.

---

47   Never say never. For as much as I love my career, if the right circumstances availed themselves to me, I'd work for Starbucks! Never say never is one important lesson in life so I can't write this chapter without this caveat.

Epilogue

When I look back at all these unique experiences, what I really want to convey is the essence of Starbucks and their unique corporate culture. The stars aligned up perfectly for there to be a StarbucksMelody.com.

For a brand to have someone writing about them like I do, there would have to be some customers who have an emotional attachment to the brand. Next, there have to be some customers who are good at writing on a regular basis. Not everyone likes to write. Importantly, there has to be a company culture where the blogger or bloggers are welcomed. A company that is threatened by someone writing about them is apt to discourage the kind of emotional loyalty that would be the prerequisite for a fan blog. To end up with experiences like you'll find in this book, you would need that blogger to be within a few miles of your headquarters.

Starbucks is unique. To have the open and welcoming culture even at very high levels of leadership is remarkable.

People have been blogging about brands for years. There's a popular blog about Trader Joe's called "What's Good at Trader Joe's.[48]" There are many Disney fan blogs. If you do some Google searching, you can find Lululemon fans blogs and Anthropologie fan blogs.

My story is unique because of these opportunities that I had with Starbucks, which would never have happened without the company culture

---

48   http://www.whatsgoodattraderjoes.com

to encourage it. Don't be afraid of your fans.

Can you imagine if some random person was a huge fan of Met Life, Wells Fargo or Pfizer, and tried to have casual, normal conversations with top executives in those companies? Can you name any other Fortune 500 company that develops a relationship with its customers like Starbucks does?

People everywhere keep returning to Starbucks because of the great experiences they're having. And on top of it, Starbucks leads in community service. Maybe I'm wrong, but I can't imagine many executive for big billion dollar corporations get down on their hands and knees and pick up litter, or plant trees in a forest.

All of this speaks to unique corporate culture of Starbucks. They convey this genuine message: *"We've got fans. We know it. We're pretty okay with that."* This book represents my stories and my experiences. I'm sure lots of people have got great Starbucks stories. And while these stories revolve around a few main characters, I'm not blind to the fact that it takes every single person who wears the green apron to bring the Starbucks experience to life.

The theme of this book, in case you missed it, was two-fold: There are great opportunities to bring people together over a cup of coffee (or tea, for that matter) and Starbucks has a uniquely human approach to doing business.

I began this book with great thanks to the many partners who bring the Starbucks experience to life, and it will end the same way.

A huge thank you to Howard Schultz and Cliff Burrows for fostering the kind of company that you do.

Bonus Story

If you liked reading about my adventures with Starbucks, please be sure to visit StarbucksMelody.com. The website address is http://www.StarbucksMelody.com

This Maple Macchiato adventure gives you an idea of the kind of tale you'll find on my site.

Maple Macchiato and the Canada Border Crossing

On a whim, I decided I would drive to Canada today (March 30, 2014). I'd gotten up early enough that I had plenty of time to make it there and back. I really wanted to try the Maple Macchiato, available only in Canada. There wasn't a lot of traffic on the road and I made good time on my journey north. However, one slow point was the border. If you don't know, you can wait twenty or more minutes. I was prepared though. I remembered my passport.

As I waited in a long lineup to pass the border patrol, I had enough time to use both my Starbucks mobile app and my in-car navigation to figure out the closest Starbucks to the border. It was (as far as I could tell) the store at 1730 – 152nd Street, South Surrey, BC.

I watched as the car immediately ahead of me went through the border crossing booth quickly. The border patrolman must have spent less than a minute on the car ahead of me. I was optimistic that I would soon be on Canadian soil.

Mr. Border Patrolman asked, "What's your business in Canada to-

day?"

I didn't have any business. "I'm just a tourist." I said, and added "Just visiting for the day."

This wasn't enough of an answer for him. I handed him my passport, as he continued to question me: "Ma'am, where are you going today?"

"I'm going to Starbucks." Apparently this wasn't enough of an answer either.

"You're going to Starbucks? I mean where specifically are you going?"

I glanced at my in-car navigation for the address: "Well, I was planning on going up to Vancouver but I don't want to drive that much. I might just go to 1730 – 152nd Street. I think it might be the Starbucks closest to the border."

Norah Jones played softly in my car. It was that CD that everyone has heard a million times, and was once sold at Starbucks.

I still had not satisfied Mr. Border Patrolman, who continued to clutch my passport. "So, you're coming to Canada to go to Starbucks?"

"Well I really want to try the Maple Macchiato. We don't have that in the United States. We got the Vanilla Macchiato instead. I thought it would be fun to try maple. I might try it and turn around and go home."

Mr. Border Patrolman lightened up a bit. "Oh yeah. I've heard about that. It's been out like three or four weeks now." At least I was talking to a fellow Starbucks customer.

"Hey, wait a minute!" Mr. Border Patrolman had this look of revelation on his face. "Are you like that guy – oh what's his name – you know the guy that's visiting every Starbucks in the world? I've seen him come through here many times, always going to Starbucks. I remember one time he told me he had to get to a store before it was closing." Mr. Border Patrolman now posed like the Thinker, with one hand on his chin, and

said *"What was his name? He's changed it before!"*

I knew he was talking about Winter[49]*. "You mean Winter? I'm friends with Winter." At this point, I hoped that there might be some beneficial guilt by association. If Winter could freely come and go to Canada, I thought I should be able to as well.*

I toyed with Mr. Border Patrolman. "Yeah, you know Winter and I are two FAMOUS customers." In reality, I don't think for a minute that there is such a thing as a "famous Starbucks customer", outside of people who are famous for other reasons and coincidentally Starbucks customers, such as Ellen DeGeneres or Sheryl Crow.

"Do you have a special routine when you go to Starbucks? I remember Winter said he has to drink at least one cup of coffee from every store he goes to."

"There's no special StarbucksMelody routine," I told him.

By this point, I was sure that the car directly behind me had to be wondering if the border patrol had done a warrant check and discovered outstanding Bench Warrants and called for local law enforcement as backup. We were taking a long time. Mr. Border Patrolman was completely nonplussed at the one mile long lineup of cars directly behind my Honda Fit.

"You know where else has a Starbucks?" Mr. Border Patrolman asked. I was tempted to reply with "everywhere" but since he was the person wearing the uniform, I opted for indulging him instead.

"Where?"

"Disneyland! I just got back from taking my family on a vacation to

---

49   Winter is a Starbucks customer on a journey to visit every single Starbucks in the world. To date, he's been to more than 11,000 Starbucks stores. He documents the stores he visits on his website, http://starbuckseverywhere.net

Disneyland, and there's a Starbucks on Main Street now!"

No wonder it takes more than 20 minutes to get through the border crossing into Canada, I thought. This conversation is never going to end. "I think that Starbucks on Main Street is probably an improvement!"

We weren't done yet. We were now approaching ten solid minutes of conversation, as I had to explain to him I had a blog too. Finally Mr. Border Patrolman said to me, "Hey, since you know Winter, have you ever seen his passport?"

"No I haven't."

"He's got this contorted expression on his face! He said he did it just to be funny! It's hilarious!"

Finally, I was allowed entry into Canada. You can't make this kind of stuff up.

I got turned around trying to get to 1730 – 152nd Street, and instead found my way to the Starbucks at <u>3288 King George Highway</u> in Surrey.

This store was decorated with balloons for the at-home coffee event sale. The register barista was asking every customer if they wanted to buy four pounds of coffee and get one free. I think I gave away that I was a tourist pretty fast. I had no Canadian money on me and so I asked the register barista if it would be okay if I tipped with American dollars. I was unsure if that was considered bad form to tip with the wrong currency. The register barista said that they'd be glad to get American dollars as tips.

"People do that all the time, since we're so close to the border." And of course, I did get my Maple Macchiato.

The cups have both French and English on them! And by the way, the tables at this Starbucks had green tablecloths on them. The Maple Macchiato was delicious. The flavor reminded of maple syrup that goes with pancakes. The lunch wraps at this Starbucks were amazing. There was a Chicken Caesar, a Thai Tuna, and a Zesty Quinoa Bean wrap. I ordered the Zesty Bean one and was impressed at how good it was. I want these wraps in the US!

This Starbucks has not converted to La Boulange food items. It's been a long time since I've looked at a non La Boulange pastry case. I was too full to buy an Oat Fudge Bar but they sure looked good.

On the drive home to Seattle, I had a long wait at the border again. I got this gorgeous photo as I sat waiting my turn to go through the border crossing.

And pretty soon I was home sweet home.

Index

Made in the USA
San Bernardino, CA
04 January 2015